The

ORVIS®

Guide to

Gunfitting

The

ORVIS®
Guide to
Gunfitting

Techniques to Improve Your Wingshooting,
and the Fundamentals of Gunfit

Tom Deck

THE LYONS PRESS
Guilford, Connecticut
An imprint of The Globe Pequot Press

The Lyons Press is an imprint of The Globe Pequot Press.

10 9 8 7 6 5 4 3 2 1

Printed in the United States

ISBN-13: 978-1-59228-216-6
ISBN-10: 1-59228-216-4

Library of Congress Cataloging-in-Publication Data is available on file.

This book is dedicated to my son, J. Hudson Deck.

"In all things of nature there is something of the marvelous."
Aristotle, *Part of Animals*

Contents

Acknowledgments

This book is the result of my ten-plus years at the Orvis Wingshooting Schools. So I must first thank all the students that I have coached over the years: You have taught me the most about what it is to be a true professional instructor. This book is as much yours as it is mine.

Thank you to all my peers and mentors at the Orvis Schools, especially Bruce Bowlen, Truel Myers, Robin Gianni, Keith Kelly, Keith Abbott, Brian Long, and Dan O'Connor. I owe a special debt of gratitude and thanks to John Rano. I especially would like to thank James Ross and Lars Jacob. I would like to thank Todd Rodgers and Bill Bowles at Winfield Plantation. A special thanks to Tom Rosenbauer. Thank you to Jordan and Skinner in the Orvis Gunsmithing department.

I owe a special thanks to my shooting mentor, Mike Wasiscko. Mike, you showed me the ropes and turned me into a professional shooting instructor. I owe you the most.

Finally, this book could not have been written without all of the help and support of my family over the years, especially that of my wife, Deborah. Thank you all very much.

The

ORVIS®

Guide to

Gunfitting

Introduction
What Is Gunfitting?

If you spend enough time beating the brush you'll make some very memorable shots. Skillful or just lucky, it doesn't matter: bird hunters often have the same stories to tell. They remember taking a grouse on opening day through thick foliage. The bird is downed amid a shower of falling leaves and splintered branches. Or there is the time they folded a teal on a long passing shot and the dog made a long, blind retrieve. These memories linger in the mind's eye, usually over a fine scotch and a halo of cigar smoke.

However, if you spend enough time in the field you will also miss a wide-open, clear, easy-as-could-be bird, when both barrels didn't so much as dust a feather. The questions start ringing in your head after missing a few easy shots. Often, one of those questions is "Does this gun fit me?"

This is a significant question and one that I believe is not explored enough by most shotgun shooters. A lot of consideration is put into what gun to buy, or what gauge is best on pheasants or quail. How well the gun fits is often mindlessly overlooked. If gun-fit is addressed at all, the stock is usually just shortened to suit a youngster or a female shooter. But stock length is only one piece of the puzzle, and in some cases adjusting the length can make problems worse. How well a gun fits can be, in fact, much more important than what type of gun to use.

A supposedly "good shot" can pick up any gun and shoot it reasonably well. This is true to some extent, because a "natural" shot can instinctively adjust to any mismatches on a particular gun stock. However, most of us do not have the eye-hand coordination to compensate for an ill-fitting gun. Through trial and error one can learn to shoot a poor-fitting gun, but to hit anything with it the shooter most likely develops bad habits, particularly with the gun mount. Whether you are a natural wingshot or a rank beginner, you will only be at your absolute best with a gun that truly fits. A fitted gun will allow you to shoot with confidence and dead-on accuracy. Shots that once required intense concentration become routine with a properly fitting gun.

Another misconception is that a shotgun is more forgiving than, say, a rifle, because of the spread, or pattern, of the shot charge, so a fitted shotgun is unnecessary. A shotgun is used on fast-moving targets that are often unpredictable. You have to swing a shotgun in an athletic motion to connect with a bird in flight. The swinging motion of a shotgun has timing and rhythm to it. A rifle shooter rarely has to move more than a few inches. More often than not you can rest a rifle steady on a stationary target and take the time to aim. There is certainly no time to adjust your aim on a grouse weaving through a stand of poplars. When you do try to aim, the result is surely a miss. So the pattern of a shotgun shell is certainly no great advantage on hard-flying birds. Robert Churchill, the famous wingshooting instructor, said it best: "A shotgun is a weapon of movement. A rifle is a weapon of immobility."[1]

What is gunfitting? It is the quest for your ideal shotgun through the process of tailoring the firearm to suit your individual build, physical features, and gun-mounting style. Bird hunters come in all shapes and sizes. This means that the average off-the-rack gun does not meet the needs of most shooters, whereas a fitted gun becomes a natural extension of a shooter's hands and eyes. The gun, primarily the stock, is tailored so that the shooter's dominant eye aligns perfectly with the sight plane of the barrels. Once the gun is mounted, the eye and the end of the gun are in perfect alignment.

When you achieve a perfect fitting there is no need to aim. You aim a rifle, but you should point a shotgun. As a bird is darting through the trees, the eye can't focus on both the barrel and the bird. Most aim a shotgun because it does not fit them. They can't trust that eye, barrel, and bird are in alignment so they check to see if everything is lined up before pulling the trigger. By aiming, the swing is interrupted and the shot is often lost behind the bird. To shoot your best, your focus must be clearly on the bird and not on the end of the gun. If your gun fits, you can lock in on your target visually without having to aim. That leads to more accurate shots and happier bird dogs.

Why is a fitted gun so important for the wingshooter? Creating a gun that shoots where your eyes are looking is critical for any serious shotgun shooter, but it is even more important for the bird hunter. Thus, gunfit is more important in wingshooting than other shooting disciplines because of the unpredictability of bird-hunting situations. Clay target games such as skeet and trap often allow you to premount the gun to the cheek and shoulder before calling for the bird. This allows a shooter to cram his head onto the stock and prearrange the gun mount so that his eye and barrel are lined up before the target takes to the air. Also when the target is launched the shooter calls for it by shouting "pull."

Furthermore, the shooter knows where the clay target is coming from and where it's going. Finally, a clay target starts fast and loses speed, while a live bird starts slow and gains speed. All of these are clear advantages the clay shooter has over the bird hunter. It would be nice if you could call for the first bird in the covey to fly out once the dog goes on point. Then each bird would fly on that same path every time you called "pull." But the challenge of bird hunting would disappear if the rules of clay shooting could be applied. So, you see, because of the unpredictability of wingshooting a premium is placed on the ability to *maintain visual contact with the bird while* mounting the gun in one fluid motion. This may sound awfully difficult to coordinate, but it is a lot easier when you do it with a fitted gun.

The Orvis company has been instrumental in touting the advantages of a bespoke gun to bird hunters. Orvis started its first shooting school in Manchester, Vermont, in 1978. This was the first organized shooting school to open its doors in America. The Orvis Wingshooting Schools have a rich history, steeped in tradition. Many generations of bird hunters have honed their skills at the Orvis shooting grounds. Grandfathers, fathers, and mothers still bring grandsons, sons, and daughters to Orvis's school to learn proper form and technique. I can remember many classes that had three generations of bird hunters from the same family in attendance. Each generation of hunters hopes that the next will learn as they did from the experts at an Orvis Shooting School. This tradition always makes me feel proud to be an Orvis instructor and I always feel a special responsibility to those students who have trusted us enough to come back over the years. As Paul Ferson wrote about Orvis, "There is no greater gift than tradition."[2] This passing of the torch allows each generation to better celebrate the sporting life.

From the very beginning, gunfit has been an integral part of the Orvis Shooting Schools. Orvis has shown countless bird hunters the importance of gunfit. The instinctive style of shooting that Orvis teaches truly shines in the field, and is most effective with a fitted shotgun. Many of our returning students understand this and credit their best days of shooting to our schools and their fitted double gun.

The Orvis schools have pioneered gunfitting in the United States. Over the years Orvis experts have fitted more than ten thousand guns. The Orvis company and its experienced gunfitters will do more fittings in one year than most instructors/gunfitters will do in a lifetime. I personally have done hundreds if not thousands of fittings during my years at the Orvis Wingshooting Schools. Thus, our extensive experience makes Orvis the perfect company to produce a book on the subject of gunfit.

So much about gunfitting has been misunderstood in America. In the United Kingdom, gunfitting has long been a part of the shotgunning culture. Understanding gunfit and how it relates to shotgunning sports is something that gun makers and instructors in England have pioneered for the rest of the world. The lack of experience in America has contributed to a certain aura of black magic around gunfitting. The inner workings of gunfit can seem complex, but the need for having a gun tailored to suit you is so basic.

Gunfit is part science and part art. The science of it is easy enough to understand as you will see in the following chapters. However, a try gun in the hands of an experienced fitter does not simply connect the dots. An expert gunfitter creates a gun that is in perfect harmony with the shooter. A properly fit shotgun can be wielded with deadly accuracy. The expert gunfitter can help you to create your ideal bird gun. Only then can you begin the search for the gun that will fit that ideal.

PART ONE

The Method

Wingshooting the Orvis Way

Seasoned wingshooters can make downing a bird seem almost effortless. They swing the gun with an easy grace, and the birds fall like sandbags from the sky. How do expert field shots make it seem so easy? Typically the only difference between the novice and the expert is that the expert has mastered the fundamentals. Wingshooting is a skill requiring timing and a bit of eye-hand coordination. You can easily learn to become a fine field shot, but like other sports it takes time. How often does an hour lesson in golf or skiing all of a sudden make you an expert?

Proper shooting technique is an important element of gunfit. That's why I feel it is important to have a section on technique in this book. An accurate fitting cannot be made until a shooter has learned to correctly handle a shotgun. A proper fitting should be done only after the shooter has developed a consistent swing and gun mount. A properly fitted stock will certainly improve your technique; however, a fitted gun is only as effective as the shooter behind it. A custom-tailored stock cannot overcome flaws in technique. Robert Churchill said it best: "Never have the stock of a gun bent or cast off to compensate for faults in gun mounting.

These should be corrected, not by deforming the gun, but by improving your style."[3]

At the Orvis Wingshooting Schools we have always taught and advocated a "modified Churchill Method" to our bird-hunting students. This method, which has evolved into what we now call the Orvis Method of Wingshooting, is based directly on the teachings of Robert Churchill. Churchill was a flamboyant character who was an expert game shot and gun builder. His teachings have been considered controversial because they are often misunderstood, in large part because of his theories on forward allowance and his preference for short-barreled guns. His teachings, however, are perfectly suited for the wingshooter, and this is why Orvis has adopted much of his techniques at our wingshooting schools.

The signature features of Churchill's method are the stylish footwork and unconscious development of the correct sight picture, or lead. He advocated a fairly narrow, square stance as a base that allows a shooter to swing and pivot freely onto either foot as the shot is taken. For a shot to the right the shooter simply swings his body, with the gun, onto the right foot and lifts the left heel. This pivot allows the body to swing freely. For a shot to the left, the body and gun would swing together and the shooter pivots onto the left foot. The right heel would then be raised, allowing the body to swing freely to the left.

In the Churchill ready position the gun is tucked up under the armpit and the muzzles held parallel to the line of sight. This ready position forces a shooter to draw the gun out toward the bird to begin the swing and mount. Also, most importantly, Churchill advocated focusing exclusively on the bird because he believed in shooting instinctively, which is to say that the eyes should be squarely on the bird and not the barrels.

Churchill's theories on developing lead are often misunderstood. As many of his supporters have stated, he did not advocate shooting at the bird. Rather, he taught that if your swing and gun mount are correct, and your focus is keenly on the bird rather than on the barrels, you would *appear* to be shooting right at the bird.

What Churchill proposes here is that the speed of the bird "compels" you to move ahead of the target by pointing with the lead hand. This is done correctly by swinging to the bird and mounting the gun in one seamless move. On short-range, or slower targets this is easy enough. On a fast, high-flying bird, though, you must move the muzzles faster in order to overtake the target, hence you will swing farther out ahead of the bird. If your eyes are on the bird then you will tend not to measure the lead with the gun barrel. This is at the heart of what Churchill meant by "shooting instinctively."

Describing the Orvis Method of Wingshooting

Like Churchill's method the Orvis Method of Wingshooting is an instinctive approach to shooting. We have made subtle modifications to Churchill's teachings over the years based on what works best in the field for our students. Most of the modifications have to do with the stance, footwork, and ready position. We recognize that the correct stance, or ready position, can depend on the build and physique of each shooter. The key fundamentals of the Orvis Wingshooting Method are Stance and Ready Position, Footwork, Swing and Gun Mount, Visual Concentration, and Gunfit. Your shooting style and your move to the bird should be built around these core components.

The Orvis method is ideal for the bird hunter because it allows one to shoot instinctively without measuring lead. The Orvis method also emphasizes pointing rather than aiming. The finest field shots harmonize the swing of the gun with the body, which makes for a smooth, dependable shooting style. Shooting instinctively is easy to appreciate when a covey busts from the brush and a pair is taken with a blast from each barrel.

The fitted gun obviously is a key component of instinctive shooting. To shoot instinctively, it's best to take the shot once the gun mount is completed to the cheek and shoulder. This becomes much easier to do if you trust that your gun is shooting where your eyes are looking. Mounting the gun too soon or staying in the gun mount too long are bad habits for the wingshooter to develop. Taking the shot as the gun mount is completed reduces any tendency to aim with the barrels. Being able to shoot instinctively and not focus on the barrels is crucial. Calculating all the different leads that one would need in the field isn't possible, and when hunting you almost never get the same shot twice. This makes it important to be able to instinctively develop a "lead" picture, a key skill that the bird hunter must develop.

So much of the instinctive shooting methods, especially Churchill's, is misunderstood and taught incorrectly. An instinctive reaction in any sport should be natural and flowing. Most shooting instruction for clays or otherwise is taught at the end of the gun. An instructor simply tells a student to have a little more lead here, and a little less lead there. This type of coaching does not help the wingshooter, because in the field no two shots are the same. This is similar to a golf coach teaching you how to play a slice instead of correcting it. "Just try to aim a little more left so that the ball slices back into the fairway" sounds reasonable until you have to play a dogleg left hole. What you need to learn is how to play the shot correctly or, in our case, how to shoot correctly. A consistent shooting style allows you develop swing by coordinating the hands, eyes, and body with the flight of the bird. All of us have the ability to point at a moving object in the sky. Combine your natural pointing ability with a gun that shoots where you're looking and you'll become a fine wingshooter in no time.

The bird hunting season can be a very diverse time of year. At the start of the season you could be hunting upland game through thick foliage, and then a few months later you could be pass shooting ducks in the wet snow of early winter. There are unique challenges to different types of bird hunting. Hunting sage grouse on the western plains is very different from shooting ducks on the eastern shore. A covey of quail is a different type of shot than a high-flying driven pheasant. For the wingshooter to be at his or her best requires a sound, instinctive technique, and, most importantly, a gun that shoots where the eyes are looking.

The Fundamentals of the Orvis Method

Stance and Ready Position

How you stand and hold the gun when awaiting the birds doesn't seem very important at first thought, but it is the very foundation of a sound shooting technique. Your stance and ready position can also affect gunfit because your stance provides stable footing, and your ready position prepares you to swing and mount the gun correctly. One of the most common faults that I see with most students is how they stand and hold the gun before they take the shot. A simple change in the stance and ready position often instantly improves a shooter's accuracy. A correct stance and ready position simply prepares you to react and move with the bird more easily. It is hard enough to connect with a shot on the wing, but it is twice as hard if you're not prepared when the bird takes

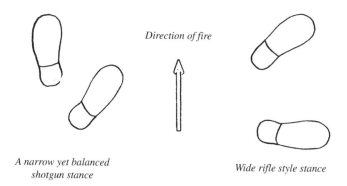

A narrow yet balanced
shotgun stance

Direction of fire

Wide rifle style stance

A) A narrow, more square shotgun stance. B) A wider, more diagonal rifle stance.

flight. All too often the novice is not properly set up when the bird flushes. From an uncomfortable position the shooter slings the gun up in an awkward attempt to catch up with the bird. If you have the correct footing and ready position when the bird appears, it's much easier to react with a smooth swing and mount.

This all sounds easy enough, but in the field time is precious. There are flushes that come without warning. You can be easily startled by a flush that catches you off guard. The bird jumps up, seemingly from right under your foot and you bumble the gun up to your shoulder, missing with both barrels. Most of the time there is ample opportunity to prepare for the shot. When the dog gets "birdy," or goes on point, that is when you begin to prepare for the flush. Even in the duck blind or dove field you can stand up in a correct position to swing and take the shot. I was hunting with my good friend who is a fine shot, and a few woodcock got up without warning from the dog. I couldn't see either of the birds as they flew. I did, however, notice that my friend brought his gun to a ready position then calmly swung onto the birds, downing one in thick cover. It really made me realize that in those first few moments when you are trying to register where the birds are there is ample time to put the gun into a ready position.

If you practice a proper ready position enough you will find that this becomes part of your gun mount. Before you begin to swing the gun onto the bird, the gun instinctively sets up in a ready position. At the Orvis Shooting Schools we sometimes create stations like a quail walk that allow our students to practice on unannounced flushes. The serious wingshooters can't seem to get enough of these stations. I have been lucky enough to hunt with some fine winghots and all of them use a proper ready position as a starting point to their gun mount.

Stance

Let us consider stance first. (I will speak in terms of a right-handed shooter. If you are a left-handed shooter as I am, then simply switch the terminology around as needed.)

There are many benefits to adopting a proper shooting stance. Understand that your stance does have an effect on how you mount the gun, so in turn, your stance does affect the fit of your gun. The correct stance sets up the body to correctly receive the gun stock for a proper mount. This will help to reduce the effects of recoil. Most importantly, a correct stance will allow the body to swing freely, while minimizing the amount of head movement. An incorrect stance makes it difficult to swing the gun without dipping the shoulders and dropping the head. Head movement is a leading cause of missed shots. In the field birds can flush or fly in any direction. The correct stance will allow you to swing the gun in harmony with the body, letting you move with the bird while minimizing head movement. So no matter which direction the bird flushes you can swing the gun smoothly on target. Remember that your stance is the foundation of your footwork, ready position, swing, and gun mount.

As a general rule a wingshooter should take as narrow a stance as possible without losing balance during the swing and mount. A narrow stance allows the wingshooter to swing more freely on unpredictable birds in the field. A narrow stance can be defined as having heels about six inches apart. This can vary a little depending on the build of the shooter. However, if the feet are held too far apart then the upper body tends to twist and the shoulders dip. This is especially true on quartering and crossing birds.

Over the years at the Orvis Wingshooting Schools our instructors have observed that the correct stance for someone can depend greatly on the build of the shooter. To simplify your setup, try to think of the lead foot as pointing in the general direction you intend to shoot. Generally speaking, though, the left foot should point at or slightly past twelve o'clock. The placement of the right foot should be pulled back a half step or two and point somewhere between two and three o'clock. Note that your stance should help to put the upper body fairly square to the line of fire. Look at the difference between a shotgun and a rifle stance, shown on page 15. A rifle stance is not acceptable for the shotgun shooter because it often puts the shoulders at a 45-degree angle for the line of fire. If the shoulders are not reasonably square to the line of fire, you are prone to mounting the butt of the gun on the upper biceps. Many rifle shooters have complained of bruising on the upper arm when handling a shotgun.

This is most often a result of adopting a rifle stance when shooting a shotgun.

Finding a comfortable stance has a lot to do with the individual build of the shooter. A tall, lean, or more flexible shooter can often take a more angled stance with the feet and still have the upper body relatively square to the target. Also a slighter shooter tends to need help soaking up recoil. By taking a less square stance with the feet, a shooter is more likely to transfer weight onto the front foot for balance. This is done with a slight forward lean during the gun mount. This shifting onto the lead foot can really help a shooter handle the recoil and shoot more comfortably. However, a more angled stance may be difficult for some body types to handle. If the upper body is angled too much from the line of fire, a mismount can result. Again, this happens when the butt of the gun is placed outside the shoulder pocket, sometimes resulting in a bruise on the upper biceps.

Your shooting stance should square the shoulders slightly to the line of fire. This will assist the shoulder pocket in receiving the butt of the gun. A shorter or more stout person may have too stiff a torso to accept the gun stock into the shoulder pocket if the stance is angled too far off the line of fire. In this case a narrower and squarer stance can really help to improve the gun mount of a less flexible shooter by squaring up the body and feet to the line of fire. The key is to adjust your stance so that it feels comfortable but still promotes a proper gun mount. Most people will feel comfortable in a narrow stance where the lead foot is pointing in the intended line of fire and the back foot pointed between two and three o'clock. This is a classic wing-shooter's stance.

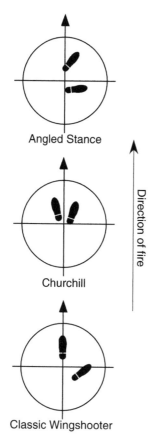

Angled Stance

Churchill

Classic Wingshooter

Direction of fire

**A) A more angled stance B) Churchill stance
C) Classic wingshooting stance**

Setting up in the right stance at the range is one thing, but then being able to apply it in the field is sometimes hard to do. If the birds get up wild or ducks dive into your decoys unannounced it can be tough to get off a good shot. However, under normal hunting circumstances there is time to at least get your stance correct before you begin your swing and mount.

Your stance and setup should allow for a slight forward lean as you mount the gun. This can be very useful to the wingshot, because it allows you to be steady on your feet. However, when the birds flush you can move slightly forward into the gun mount. This can help you move to the bird and absorb recoil. This little forward lean actually makes it easier to mount the gun correctly. The weight should shift onto the straight but not stiff front leg, with the head moving ever so slightly forward. The little forward head movement makes it easier to lift the gun and raise the stock to the cheek. If you can keep the chin up during the forward lean, you will

avoid dropping the head to meet the stock. This subtle leaning action will make raising the gun up to cheek and shoulder with minimal head movement much easier. If your eyes remain steady so will
your aim. Once again, the correct stance should allow for a subtle
weight transfer onto the lead foot. I can't begin to tell you how many
students comment on how that little forward lean helps them move
with the bird and mount the gun so easily.

How does your stance affect the fit of your gun? Stance can
have a direct effect on the length of pull of your gun stock. A more
angled stance often allows for a longer length of pull. Angling the
upper body away from the line of fire pulls the shoulder pocket
back allowing a shooter to soak up more gun. Many people come
to a wingshooting school with considerable rifle shooting experience. When they set up in their rifle shooting stance they often
complain that the gun we gave them feels awkwardly short.
Sometimes this is true. However, most of the time their rifle
stance has their upper body angled too far off from the line of fire.
By simply adjusting the setup so that the feet are squarer to the
target, the stock feels much longer. A squarer stance tends to face
the upper body and shoulders more to the line of fire. This typically shortens the length of pull needed for a given shooter. The
key here is to adopt a stance that helps reduce recoil and makes
it easy to find the shoulder pocket without having to drop the
head down to meet the comb. A stance that is too square will
sometimes not allow for a proper weight transfer. If the feet are
set up too square this can make it difficult to lean on the lead foot
during the swing and mount. A shooter with a stance that is too
square can have trouble handling recoil and is often off balance
when shooting. The lead foot should be comfortably set ahead of

The head should remain steady as you lean slightly forward to complete the gun mount.

Your stance can affect the fit of your gun, particularly the length of pull: notice how long the gun seems in the first picture and how short it looks in the second.

a slightly angled back foot. This setup allows you to be in balance as you shift your weight onto the front foot. Examine your stance and adjust it accordingly so that you are in balance and mounting the gun smoothly.

Ready Position

One of the first steps in gunfitting is to develop a consistent and repeatable gun mount. A consistent swing and gun mount allows a shooter to bring the gun up to the shoulder and head the same way each time. The key to these talents is to have a set ready position to begin from. As stated before, the ready position should become part of your gun mount. Without a set ready position the gun is slung up from a host of different holding positions. If no two starting positions are the same then most likely no two gun mounts will be the same either. A proper ready position will help to simplify your swing and gun mount. It will allow your body to develop muscle memory, so you can have a repeatable gun mount that you can trust. The more trust you have in your gun mount, the more you'll be able to focus on the bird without worrying if the eye is in alignment with the barrel. The whole concept of gunfit is based around mounting the gun consistently. A default ready position will help to simplify your swing and gun mount for repeatable success.

Bird hunters often have no recollection of how the gun was held prior to the bird flushing. Most shots are taken from what is called "the hunting position." The hunting position may be an effective way to walk through the woods, but it is a terrible ready position to have to shoot from. In the hunting position the stock is held near the hip with the barrels pointing to the sky. This makes it easy for a hunter to weave through the thick foliage of a bird covert. However, think about how difficult it is to connect from the hunting position with a ground-flushed bird. From the hunting position the barrels are hatchet-chopped downward from the sky to connect with a bird that is typically rising off the forest floor. The shooter swings the barrels down in an attempt to connect with a rising target.

Also note that a proper ready position can be safer when approaching a dog with a hunting partner at your side. A good friend

This shooter has an attentive ready position prior to the covey flush.

of mine, Todd Rodgers, a professional hunting guide, will often have his shooters take a correct ready position once his dogs go on point. In the ready, the barrels are held out in front of each shooter. This will avoid anyone walking up to the dog with the gun held across the chest. If you are on the left side of the dog and your shooting partner is right-handed then the last thing you want is your hunting partner's gun barrels tilting your way. If both shooters walk up to the birds in a proper ready position, the barrels will be safely pointing downrange. Not only is this safer, but it makes it easier to begin your swing and mount.

Whenever possible, adopt a safe and proper ready position before you attempt to mount the gun. Birds can be unpredictable, and it's impossible to walk all day in the field with the gun in the alert position. There are certain types of bird hunting that provide a better opportunity for establishing a ready position than others.

The ready position (above) is a much better starting point than the hunting position (below).

If you hunt upland game over pointing dogs there can be ample time to set up for the flush. Once the dogs go on point, abandon the hunting position and place the gun in a proper ready position, so as you approach the dogs your gun will be in a much better position to shoot from. Even if you upland hunt with flushing dogs, you will see clearly when the dogs are getting birdy—just take care to look for changes in the dogs' body language as they pick up the scent of a grouse or pheasant. The tail might start wagging faster, and the nose usually drops closer to the ground. Over time the exact moment when you should adopt the ready position will become quite apparent, because a bird might bust at any moment. I had a friend whose retriever would make loud puffing grunts of air when it got a nose full of bird scent. Once he heard that he'd say, "Get ready," because you knew a bird was going to soon flush.

Even when pass shooting on ducks or doves you can develop somewhat of a ready position prior to taking the shot. If you're sitting in a duck blind try to prepare yourself so that you can stand up into a correct ready position as you begin mounting the gun. This is easier said than done, but taking the time to swing the gun from a ready position will help you judge the line and speed of the bird better. Many duck hunters make the mistake of mounting the gun as soon as they stand up. If you mount the gun prematurely as you stand you will have trouble maintaining the momentum needed to connect with hard-flying birds. Taking a ready position will force you to swing with the bird before shouldering the gun. The field gunner with a correct ready position is certain to make the best swing and gun mount possible, under very unpredictable hunting conditions.

I hope that I have convinced you of the need for a ready position. Now let's establish how to hold the gun prior to the swing and gun mount.

Swing and Gun Mount

The Ready Position Further Defined

The ready position is the starting point of your swing and gun mount. The ready position should be a comfortable and fundamentally sound way to hold the gun prior to making your move to the bird. In the correct ready position your gun is held with the muzzles just below the line of sight, with the stock tucked comfortably under the armpit. The gun is at an angle so that the barrels are up slightly. However, the stock definitely should not hang loosely below the right forearm. The right arm should gently hug the stock next to the upper chest and ribs. The left or lead hand should be extended on the forend to enhance your ability to point at the bird. Many shooters will extend the index finger along the barrels to further heighten their pointing instincts. From this basic setup let's explore the subtleties of a correct ready position.

Each hand has a purpose while holding the gun in the ready. The right arm should hold the gun snugly next to the body. This can help support the weight of the gun and barrels on the left hand. Also allow the shoulders to be relaxed and the body to stand tall as you await the birds to take flight. Try to have only $1\frac{1}{2}$ or 2 inches of the butt stock tucked under the armpit. Starting with a little bit of the butt stock under the armpit forces you to push the gun out toward the bird. When the gun is held under the armpit you can't

The correct ready position has the stock tucked comfortably under the armpit. And the barrel is held just below the line of sight.

simply lift the stock to the shoulder. You must first push it out toward the bird to begin the swing and mount. This is an important element to consider. The wingshooter needs to be able to point at the bird while mounting the gun. If the gun is correctly placed in the ready it should simplify the swing and mount.

The finest wingshooters use the leading hand on the forearm to point out the target during the swing and mount. The placement of the lead hand should enhance your ability to move or swing in harmony with the bird. Remember that you aim a rifle but point a shotgun. The Orvis method is based on the natural pointing ability that all of us have. Pick a spot on the wall and point at it. Notice how your hand reaches out and the arm is straightened somewhat. This is how the lead hand should handle a shotgun.

Also by starting with the stock slightly under the armpit you are compelled to move out to the bird with the lead hand during the gun mount. I have seen this ready position work wonders for many shooters. I once had a student named Darren who was one of the most naturally gifted wingshooters I had ever taught. He came to the Orvis Shooting School for an odd problem. Darren could easily knock off the hardest targets, but he had a heck of a time shooting a basic going-away or quartering shot. Darren talked passionately about his love for dove and quail hunting. He told me that the easiest of quail flushes gave him fits, but he always took his limit of dove well before any of his hunting buddies. Darren and his friends were always shocked when he struggled on basic upland shots. After seeing him miss a few easy clay targets it was clear to see that the problem was his ready position. He held the stock so low and loosely that the gun seesawed up and down as he took his mount. This problem was more pronounced on the easier straightaway and quartering targets. Also this problem was compounded by the fact that Darren was extremely right-hand-dominant and shot off of his right shoulder. His right hand was overpowering his left. I adjusted his ready position, and he made an instant improvement.

I had him hold his barrels lower so that they were just below his line of sight. What really helped him the most, however, was tucking a little of the stock up under the armpit, because that forced Darren to draw the gun out toward the bird more with the left hand. This reduced the right hand's tendency to overpower and create a seesaw gun mount. The simple adjustment of Darren's ready position smoothed out his swing and really improved his shooting on those easier targets. His buddies in his shooting group weren't pleased with his new style because they couldn't cut him up over missing the easy ones anymore.

Darren's problem was not unique. Most right-handed shooters are naturally right-handed, which makes perfect sense. This makes the left hand the leading or pointing hand. For a person who is strongly right-handed this can often create the seesaw gun mount, when the dominant right hand lifts the stock up to the shoulder much of the left hand can track the bird. The stock is mounted to the shoulder prematurely and the barrels have trouble catching up to the bird. Shouldering the gun prematurely also produces a greater tendency to aim. In short, if the hands work independently, the shooter is often out of rhythm with the bird. By tucking a little of the butt stock under the armpit you are forced to draw the gun out to begin the swing and mount. This can help the left hand move with the bird while the right hand is moving the stock up to the shoulder and cheek. By tucking the gun under the armpit you are forced to push the gun out rather than simply lifting the stock with the right hand.

How high the muzzle is held with the left hand is also very important. It is best to hold the muzzle a little below the line of sight when bird hunting. This allows you to get a clear view of the bird so you can still point and swing the gun on target. Most bird hunting situations are unpredictable, so it is imperative that your view is unobstructed by the barrels as you start the gun mount.

The best bird shots are the ones that happen instinctively. The bird seems to fall in one clean shot without your having any recollection of aiming. When you aim, the swing is interrupted because the eye can't focus on the barrels and the bird. By holding the barrels below the line of sight you can point and swing with the bird instinctively. This also creates fewer tendencies to aim because the muzzle is not directly in the sight line. By holding the gun in the correct ready position you are compelled to make the best swing and gun mount possible while keeping your focus on the birds.

Your natural pointing instincts are the very heart of successful wingshooting. How you hold the gun should help to accentuate your natural pointing ability. The placement of the leading left hand on the forend to point to a bird in flight should be as natural and fluid as pointing to a spot on the wall.

Try this experiment to establish where the left hand should grip the forend: look at a spot on the wall. Point at it with your left hand and then turn over your hand and imagine placing the forend of the gun in your palm. Notice that you extended the left arm until it is nearly straight. This is how we all tend to point at something. Next time you see some songbirds flying by, point at them with your left hand. Then notice the position of the left arm. This nearly straight

Thick cover can create difficulties for your stance, but keeping your muzzle a little below the line of sight is essential. This will help you to get a clearer view of the flush.

arm is how you should hold the gun. Often the lead hand is too far back on the forend. This creates an excessive bend in the elbow, like that of a rifle shooter. Having a little more bend in the elbow is often the choice of many clay shooters and it can be effective on predictable targets. But it's unnatural to point accurately with an excessive bend in the elbow. As a wingshooter you want to be able to react instinctively to hard-flying, unpredictable birds. Pointing and swinging the gun effectively can't happen with the hand too far back on the forend. You want your first reaction to be your best, and the most effective way is to point naturally at the bird.

The pointer finger of the left hand can actually extend along the side of the forend of an over-under to enhance the act of pointing. On a side-by-side many shooters will extend the index

The best way to swing and point out a bird is with a nearly straight left arm.

finger between the barrels on the underside of the gun. (The splinter forend of a side-by-side was originally designed to hold the gun together rather than to encourage the placement of the hand. Often the thumb and first two fingers will extend out beyond the forend and grip the barrels of a side-by-side.) Make sure that the thumb and fingers rest along the barrels and not over the rib. This would seem like common sense, but I have seen many experienced wingshooters block out part of their field of vision by holding a thumb or finger dangerously close to the rib. This is especially true of side-by-side shooters.

The lead hand should cradle the forend, with the fingers comfortably spread apart along the gun rather than on top of the barrels. The forend should also be held more with the fingers than with the palm of the hand. Avoid a heavy-handed grip where the forend rests deeply in the palm, and the fingers encroach the rib.

Take care to hold the gun carefully, but do not grip the forend forcefully. The grip of the lead hand should be light, as if you could slide the gun easily back and forth through the fingers, but the grip should also naturally tighten as the shot is taken. This along with an extended elbow will not only help your swing, but it can reduce felt recoil on the shoulder.

The left hand would seem to do the bulk of the work, but actually the hands need to work together to successfully swing and mount the gun. The left hand should point out the bird as the right lifts the stock up to the head and shoulder. The fingers of the right hand should wrap around the grip, with the index finger extended along the side of the trigger guard. In the ready position the index finger should never come in contact with the trigger and should stay on the trigger guard until the end of the swing and gun mount. A paramount rule is that the index finger should touch the trigger when the shot is going to be fired only, never before taking the shot. The thumb should rest on the safety in the off position, and then wrap around the grip as the safety is disengaged. The safety should come off as you begin your swing onto the bird. When this is done correctly it automatically becomes part of your swing and gun mount. Be sure to slide the thumb off the top of the receiver after the safety is taken off. I have seen many a thumb bashed open by the top tang recoiling into it as the shot was fired. Also make sure not to overrotate the grip of your right hand around the stock. This will cause the elbow to rise up uncomfortably as you mount the gun. Also, by overgripping with the right hand you are prone to bruising your middle finger on the back of the trigger guard as the shot is fired.

Music, like shooting, has a rhythm to it. A concert violinist's hands appear to work independently, but together they create

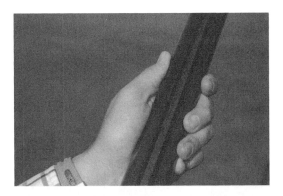

The proper way to hold a side-by-side is to make sure the thumb and fingers rest along the barrels and not over the rib. Some shooters extend the index finger under the barrels to enhance their pointing ability. You can also extend the index finger alongside the forend on an over-under.

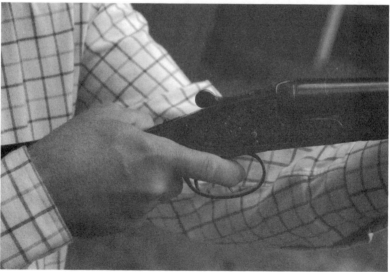

The finger should rest along the trigger guard and remain there as you swing the gun. Only the tip of the finger should touch the trigger when you are ready to fire.

beautiful music. The shooter's mount and swing is like a duet of the hands, each playing their part in rhythm with the bird. When done correctly the hands swing the gun in one harmonious and rhythmic movement to take the bird on the wing. This rhythm begins by setting up in the correct ready position prior to moving with the bird.

Footwork

Drawing a shotgun onto a fast-moving target is a dynamic movement, and footwork is the foundation of proper technique. If your footwork is solid then your swing and mount will seem smooth and easy. If your setup and footwork are poor it can make shooting seem awkward and clumsy. The unpredictability of bird hunting places a premium on having the correct footwork and setup. A clay shooter has time to establish a break point and then adjust the stance and footwork to help make the shot easier. In the field this can be difficult and sometimes impossible to do.

An experienced field shot, however, possesses footwork that allows the body to swing freely with the bird. Picking the exact spot where you want to shoot a bird, before the bird flushes, is very tricky and often next to impossible. For this reason you need to develop the proper footwork that will allow the body to swing beyond any preconceived "break point." Your footwork and setup will establish how well the body can swing the gun in concert with the bird. An incorrect setup will lead to an awkward shot. The right footwork helps the body to smoothly mount the gun. The right footwork should enhance your pointing ability and improve your overall style in the field.

The best footwork should allow you to swing your gun freely on even the most unpredictable birds because establishing the

The proper wingshooting footwork should allow you to pivot onto either foot.

correct stance and setup allows a shooter to pivot and shoot off of either foot. This gives the shooter a larger window of opportunity to swing onto the bird. With proper foot placement the feet and body are relatively square to the line of fire. This setup has the heels no more than six inches apart. If possible, point your lead foot toward your intended line of fire. Set the feet as close together as possible without compromising balance. This may be just inside of shoulder width. A narrow stance will allow a shooter to transfer weight onto either foot with greater ease and less head movement. If the stance is too wide the body will twist uncomfortably and a proper pivot cannot be made. The beauty of such wingshooting footwork is that if the bird flies off course your body should be able to swing in either direction to take the shot. Remember, the shotgunner's stance and setup is very different from the rifle shooter's. The wingshooter wants a squarer stance so that the upper body can receive the gun in a proper mount.

A shot moving right to left is the natural swing for a right-hander. The weight will shift onto the left foot and the right heel should rise off the ground. The farther left the swing takes you the more the right heel should clear the ground. How much the heel clears the ground can depend on the angle of the bird, the shooter's build, and foot placement.

The correct wingshooters' footwork allows for many overhand and crossing shots to be taken off the right foot. For a shot to the right, the weight should transfer onto the right foot as the body swings with the bird. Now the left heel will clear the ground as the swing moves onto the right side. Again make sure you have a narrow enough stance to allow a balanced weight transfer. When done correctly your upper body should swing freely to the bird, and the shoulders should be parallel to the ground. Pivoting onto the right foot will seem awkward at first for the right-handed shooter, but with some practice it can be effective.

Advice for the Wingshooter

Refining Stance and Footwork

For most wingshooters the correct stance and footwork can vary a little depending on the build and body type of each shooter. In our years of coaching shooters at the Orvis schools we have come to understand that each person is unique. The build and flexibility of a person can dictate how square a hunter can stand to the line of fire. (To review, see pp. 16–27 on stance and ready position.)

For some shooters, standing too square to the line of fire can be very awkward. This is particularly true on a straightaway bird or a direct incomer. This creates an unbalanced shot because there is no clear foot to pivot onto. Hence it is hard to lean into the shot, making it difficult to absorb recoil. However, how often do birds fly straightaway or come directly overhead? For most shooters, shifting the weight or transferring balance onto the right foot can cause the shoulders to tilt unnaturally at the end of the swing. This leads to dropping the head, making it hard to follow the true flight line of the bird. In a perfect world every shot would allow you to lean slightly forward onto the lead foot. This will help your mount and allow you to soak up recoil.

All this aside, there are times when a bird will surprise you, and there is no time to adjust your foot placement. When this happens the best field shooters know how to swing and shoot off of the opposite foot. Like most techniques you might not use them all the time, but to shoot your best you need to adapt your style to suit the situation. This type of footwork can also be useful for a shooter with a shorter, thicker build. A more stout shooter may have limited rotation between the upper and lower body, so transferring the weight onto either foot can allow the upper body to move freely as one unit. This footwork also can be helpful when caught off guard by a bird flying at a difficult angle. I must admit that the first grouse I shot came off a pivot onto my off foot just as Robert Churchill prescribed.

This type of footwork was developed mostly for driven shooting. On a driven shoot you have time to prepare for the birds as they fly overhead. Also there are well-defined shooting boundaries that limit how far one should swing and shoot. The serious wingshooter should learn to adapt his or her stance and footwork to suit the different types of bird hunting. Upland hunting is certainly different from shooting waterfowl. Your stance and footwork will vary depending on the situation.

Most shooters adopt what is called the wingshooter's stance and shoot off of the lead foot on most predictable birds. This tends to work best for most shooters, especially if there is time to get the feet set prior to beginning the gun mount. Adjustments can be made in this stance according to the shot being taken. For example, if you're a right-hander and you know the shot has to be a left to right, then you can place the left foot in position to allow more swing to the right. This is helpful if you're upland hunting with a partner and you are on the right side of the dog. In this case you will have all the birds that flush to the right of the working dog. Also, if you're duck hunting, you can stand up onto the lead foot for birds flying hard to the right. As you stand up, place the lead foot more to the right to allow for a right-to-left swinging bird.

There will be circumstances when you're caught off guard and you really don't have time to adjust the stance. Part of the excitement of hunting is that you can't predict how the birds will fly. On these surprise shots there is no time to take the shot off of the left foot. In this case you should learn to pivot onto the right foot and free up the body for a left-to-right swing. Being able to adapt your stance and footwork for a given hunting situation will truly improve your overall shooting and success in the field.

Refining Swing and Gun Mount

To thoroughly use a fitted gun one should develop a consistent swing and gun mount. A properly fitted stock will shoot straight provided that the gun is mounted the same way each time to the shoulder and cheek. If the gun is mismounted then the eye-barrel relationship is off and the benefits of the gunfit exponentially decrease the farther away the bird is. A mismount at twenty-five yards often leads to a crippled bird, and the dog often has a hard time finding it. Also that same mismount on a forty-yard bird is probably a clean miss. So to really reap the full benefit of a custom-tailored stock you first must develop a consistent swing and gun mount. This is at the heart of the shooting technique taught in this book.

The swing and gun mount are key components to a successful shooting style and should be one harmonious movement of the feet, hands, body, and head. Swinging with a bird in flight and mounting the gun must not be two separate acts. Correct shooting style incorporates swing as part of mounting the gun.

The novice, however, often separates mounting and swinging the gun, usually by shouldering the stock first and then attempting to swing the barrels and lock onto the bird visually. This is poor technique for many reasons. For one, picking up the target visually if you have the gun fully mounted before the bird comes into clear view is difficult. In essence, the receiver and gun barrel obstructs part of your field of vision when in the mounted position. Trying to locate a flushing grouse with a gun up in your face is even harder in thick cover. I have seen many shooters who fully mount the gun even before they see the birds; they hear the flush, and then they whip the stock up to the shoulder and feverishly wave the barrels around trying to locate the birds in the air. The covey busts left and the shooters point right, never really seeing where the birds flew.

The gun mount should begin only when you clearly see the bird. For the experienced shooter in the field, all the elements instinctively come together to produce an effective swing and mount. Once the dog becomes birdy, or goes on point, become alert. Even if you are caught off guard, you can still use the proper technique. Often an upland hunter will hear the flush before seeing the bird because of thick cover or brush. When you hear the busting of the bird there is time to set the feet and drop the gun into a ready position. The ear picks up the noise of the bird flushing. The body and eyes naturally turn to pick the target. Only then is the gun smoothly raised to the shoulder in coordination with the flight path of the bird. This reaction will begin to happen instinctively with more field experience.

As we've discussed, to complete the swing and mount, lift the gun as one unit without much hinging action—that is, the gun should rise along a level plane. The barrels should come up to the bird at about the same time the butt of the gun reaches the shoulder and cheek. Many instructors use the image of a glass of scotch resting on the rib of the gun. During the swing and mount they say, "Don't spill the scotch." This is something that Robert Churchill recommended. You can't take this analogy literally on some angles like an overhead shot, but it does paint a picture.

When I'm teaching wingshooters, I often try to have them use what I call "the flashlight mount." Hold the tip of the barrel below the line of sight. A more experienced shooter may hold the stock

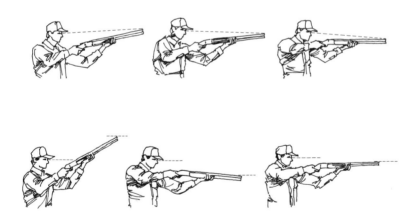

A) The flashlight swing and mount has barrels pointing directly along the same flight path as the bird, eyes aligned with the muzzle. B) At all costs avoid a seesaw swing and mount in which each hand moves too independently, putting the eyes and muzzle out of alignment. (See bottom photo, p. 48, for completed mount position.)

at elbow level at address. I recommend that new shooters tuck the stock more up under the armpit to emphasize thrusting out at the bird. The idea of the flashlight mount is to imagine a focused beam of light streaming out of the barrels, directed by the lead hand. As the mount begins, imagine your beam of light staying on the same flight line as the bird. For a straightforward shot, see the beam staying right on the bird as you raise the gun up to your cheek and shoulder. On a longer crossing shot, envision the beam of light drawing ahead of the bird as you complete the swing and mount. This flashlight mount makes it easy to swing in line with the bird, and avoid misses high or low. Also, this imagery instills the idea of pointing or putting the barrels on the bird with the lead hand as the swing and mount begins. This often slows down the shooter and avoids prematurely mounting the gun to the shoulder.

Skilled field shooters will harmonize the swing and mount by the use of the hands. The hands need to work together, otherwise problems can arise if they don't. One of the most common gun-mounting faults I see is an overpowering right hand. This creates a seesaw gun mount because the stock is raised up to the shoulder before the barrels align with the bird. Most people shooting off of the right shoulder are right-handed, so they tend to be more aggressive at lifting the gun up to the shoulder and cheek. This will cause the stock to come up ahead of the barrels, producing a miss low. I'm sometimes guilty of the opposite of this problem. I'm a natural right-hander, but I shoot off of the left side. My pointing, or lead, hand is my right. At times an overpowering lead hand makes my barrels come up to the target before the gun is fully mounted. This can create a miss that is high.

If the hands are working together correctly the lead hand should point out the bird as the right hand slowly lifts the stock up into the shoulder and cheek. The left hand leads the muzzle up to the bird by pointing where the eyes are looking. The lead hand should draw the gun out in a smooth, thrusting move toward the bird. The right hand assists by raising the gun up to the shoulder and helps the lead hand track the bird.

During the swing and mount, keep your head steady. In the heat of the moment there is a temptation to drop the head down to meet the stock. This is a common mistake and another leading cause of misses. But you can't focus on the bird if your head is dropping down during the mount. So minimizing head movement is critical to effective shooting. The proper head movement is ever so slightly forward during the gun mount and swing. Slightly moving the head forward makes it easier to accommodate the stock up into the cheek. To avoid dropping the head think of keeping your chin up as you lean slightly forward into the shot. By keeping your head up you are forced to raise the stock up to your cheek. This will minimize head movement and allow you to focus squarely on the bird. Also, leaning into the shot will help the momentum of your swing and reduce the effects of recoil.

To complete the mount the right hand will slide the stock up to your head and your shoulder will actually come forward to meet the butt. If you have to bring the stock back to the shoulder this will disrupt your swing. This is what happens if the length of pull is too short (we'll discuss length of pull and other gun dimensions later). The right hand should place the stock up into the fleshy part of the cheek so that there is some jowl hanging over the comb. This will protect the cheekbone from bruising as the shot is fired. Again, if your hands work together this will help to reduce felt recoil. The lead hand should naturally tighten as the shot is taken, which will help to reduce the recoil into the shoulder. At the same time, the right hand should place the stock into the fleshy part of the cheek to keep the gun from jarring the cheekbone.

A gun mount is an attempt to put the barrels and the eyes in alignment. You are not trying to line the barrels up with your shoulder. But a novice shooter frequently puts the butt of the gun into the shoulder pocket before the comb reaches the cheek. Doing so forces the shooter to drop the head down to the comb. This is an awkward way to mount the gun and the excessive head drop makes focusing on the bird a lot harder. Remember that you are trying to bring the gun up to your line of sight, so mounting the gun to the cheek makes perfect sense. If you mount the gun into the cheek properly the butt stock seats perfectly into the shoulder pocket every time. This is especially true if the stock fits correctly.

Try this little experiment: take your gun from the correct ready position and smoothly mount the gun by concentrating on pressing the comb into the fleshy part of your cheek. You should notice that the gun comes up to your head and that the butt lands neatly into the shoulder pocket. This creates a smooth gun mount without dropping your head down to meet the gun. Also the butt of the gun meets the shoulder pocket without any awkward adjustments. The better your gun fits, the easier this little drill becomes.

Making your swing and mount slow and smooth is crucial. The more you rush the gun mount into the shoulder pocket the more the lead hand loses pace with the bird. The lead hand should start

Keep your head up as you lean slightly forward to complete the mount. This will force you to lift the gun up without dropping the head down to meet the stock.

the swing by drawing the gun out toward the bird. The right hand should raise the gun smoothly to the shoulder and cheek without disrupting the pointing action of the left hand. If the gun is slung up abruptly, this destroys the rhythm of your swing. Developing a smooth and effective pointing hand without rushing the gun mount will actually make most shooters quicker in the field. Shooting quickly in the field is a product of the left hand pointing out the bird before the stock is placed in the mounted position. This allows the barrel to align with the birds without having to purposely aim once the gun is brought to the shoulder and cheek, reducing the tendency to stop the swing and "aim" down the barrels. The shot follows naturally.

Remember that the whole purpose of a fitted gun is that it will shoot wherever the eyes are looking. If you stop and "check your aim," then most likely your swing will slow down. To help avoid this it is best to take the shot once the gun is fully mounted. If your eyes are squarely focused on the target and the gun is mounted, then there is nothing left to do but pull the trigger. Hesitation at this point of the swing and mount can only cause problems. The seasoned wingshot seems to swing, mount, and fire the gun in one seamless flow. Once you develop a consistent swing and gun mount you will truly reap the benefits of a fitted stock.

Visual Concentration

One of the most useful skills a successful wingshooter develops is unwavering visual concentration on the bird. You must develop an ability to clearly focus on the bird without being distracted by trees or the gun barrel. The level of visual concentration often is what separates a memorable shot from a humiliating miss. This is without a doubt one of the key fundaments of wingshooting. Visual concentration is not to be confused with visual acuity. Seeing well and concentrating well are two different issues.

When shooters lapse in concentration during a coaching session, I will ask them what they saw when they pulled the trigger. The answer is almost always, "I really don't know." Typically on a miss a shooter sees everything. He sees the trees, clouds, gun barrel, and maybe a glimpse of the target. Unfortunately, the target was a blur against a panoramic backdrop. The correction for this type of miss on most quartering and going-away shots is

To see this covey bust from thick cover you need unwavering visual concentration.

to simply look for some detail on the target. Focus on the rings or the leading edge of the clay, rather than blankly looking at the whole target. There is a huge difference between looking at the whole target and clearly focusing on a piece of the target.

Intense visual concentration can happen naturally in the field. The game is flushed and before you know it the bird is falling end over end after you pull the trigger. You don't recall the background or even remember seeing the gun barrel. These types of shots are a product of visual concentration. Examples of such concentration are seeing the white ring around the neck pheasant without noticing much else of the bird, or clearly "picturing the lead" on a wood duck before pulling the trigger without focusing on the nearby trees.

Your level of visual concentration has nothing to do with how well you see. Having 20/20 vision certainly helps, but focusing intently on the bird can be done even through the thickest corrective lenses. Focus comes from mental concentration. Remembering to pick out the head of one quail rather than shooting at the whole covey takes concentration. Have you ever had a day of shooting where you were just on? Your gun mount and swing were effortless and smooth. Your confidence was sky high and the birds seem to just fall when the trigger was pulled. You knew you were going to hit the target even before the gun was fully mounted. This was because you were in a zone of concentration that couldn't be broken.

Athletes peaking at their best enter what they call "the zone." How does one get into the zone? Through practice the correct muscle memory is built. Once the movement, or in our case, the swing, is mastered, getting into the zone takes place through concentration. The zone is described as a high level of mind and body awareness whereby things appear to be moving in slow motion and our reactions seem effortless. By effortless I don't mean to imply that one is not trying. Rather, the shooter becomes so committed and focused on the target that the body reacts in perfect harmony with the eyes. The focus of the mind and the reaction of the body become one effortless stream of consciousness. You're not thinking about the gun or your swing. You don't see the trees or clouds as the bird takes flight. Your concentration is completely on the target, which is where it should be. Remember, to perform your best during the hunting season it helps to practice at the range. Once your swing and mount are committed to muscle memory, you free your mind to focus exclusively on the target. Practice the fundaments of shooting but also work on heightening

Heightened visual concentration allows shooters to be at their best.

Where should your focus be as you are going to take the shot?

your focus on the target so when that first bird of the year takes off you can see the feathers on its neck.

Concentration on the target is made easier with the use of a fitted gun. The concept of a custom stock allows you to heighten your focus on the bird because the gun will point wherever the eyes are looking. As the gun mount is completed and the shot is taken all you need to do is keep your focus squarely on the bird. The more trust you have in your gun mount and stock dimensions, the easier focusing on the bird becomes. Remember that the whole idea of visual concentration is that you can't hit something without clearly looking at it. This might all seem very obvious, but focusing on your target visually can be easily taken for granted. Shooting at the whole bird is a world apart from focusing on its head before pulling the trigger. I will talk more about visual concentration in the next chapter, "The Sight Picture and Forward Allowance."

Defining Eye Dominance

Eye dominance is an interesting and important subject to the gunfitter and shooter alike. You should fully understand how eye dominance affects your shooting before you invest in a custom gun. For most of us, shooting with both eyes open is a distinct advantage because this allows you to use binocular vision. You can judge the speed, distance, and flight line of the bird more effectively. However, many people simply cannot shoot their best with both eyes open and need to make allowances for eye dominance issues.

The dominant eye controls the pointing action of the hands. For the most part, only one eye controls this pointing action. If you point at a leaf on a tree, the eye that lines up with the end of your finger is considered dominant. This is also true with the eye that lines up with the end of the gun as you complete the gun mount. Interestingly, eye dominance does not relate to which eye actually sees better. You can have stronger vision in your left eye and still be right-eye dominant. Also, the dominant eye is not always clear-cut for everyone. There are varying degrees or different types of eye dominance.

A person who has one "strongly dominant" eye means that the pointer finger and this eye directly line up. A strongly dominant-eyed person has a direct line between one eye, the tip of the gun, and the bird. If you shoot off of the right shoulder and you have a strongly dominant right eye then you can most likely shoot with both eyes open.

A person can also have a "weakly dominant" eye. This is when the eye and pointer finger might line up, but this can easily change because of other factors. A weakly dominant eye does not truly have total control of the pointing action of the hands. Factors like stress, lack of sleep, or peering into a computer screen for hours can all affect the weakly dominant-eyed shooter. If you are a right-handed shooter and have a weakly dominant eye, then the finger or the gun barrel might not line up perfectly. In this case the shooter must accommodate by closing the left eye prior to finishing the gun mount, or using a piece of tape on the shooting glasses. There are easy ways to remedy eye dominance problems, and I will cover that shortly.

A shooter can also be "cross-dominant." This is when a shooter's master eye is opposite the shoulder he or she shoots from. Very often a person can be right-handed and have a left master eye. When a wingshooter is strongly cross-dominant, the best bet is often to learn to shoot off of the other shoulder. For someone who is extremely left-eye dominant, but right-handed, shooting off of the left shoulder can be much more effective than trying to shoot right-handed. Switching shoulders may not be for everyone, but for the new, untrained shooters who are strongly cross-dominant the switch can work beautifully.

Some people have what is known as "central vision." This is when neither eye is dominant. When a person with central vision points at something the finger lines up directly in between both eyes. In this case, each eye is of equal strength and neither takes total control of pointing. The gun barrel tends to line up directly in the middle of the eyes as the mount is completed. Some shooters have their stocks altered to compensate for central vision or

This shooter is most likely right-eye dominant.

Here he seems to have central vision.

This is how the gun lines up on a shooter who is clearly cross-dominant.

cross-dominance. For shooters who are extremely cross-dominant, and wouldn't dream of switching shoulders, a crossover stock can be made. Such a stock has an extreme bend so the butt remains on the shoulder but the barrels curve over to the opposite eye. A similar but less extreme bend can be made to help a shooter with central vision. These stock configurations are increasingly rare these days. Before you invest in this expensive and gangly stock consult a professional gunfitter. There are many other effective alternatives you should exhaust before undertaking such an extreme stock makeover.

Eye Dominance and Your Shooting

How does eye dominance affect your shooting? This is a good question because eye dominance can significantly change where your shotgun patterns. Let's say that you shoot off of your right shoulder, but you're left-eye dominant. This can cause your gun to pattern significantly to the left. This happens because the left eye wants to direct the end of the gun. Even though the stock is on the right shoulder the barrels line up with the left eye. You are looking directly at the target, but the left eye pulls the barrels slightly to the left. (This assumes that both eyes are open when you shoot.) The more dominant the off eye is, typically the more your gun will pattern off center. A shooter who is extremely cross-dominant can even have difficulty mounting the gun correctly. Often the head will cant over the stock so that the left eye peers down the barrel. Even if a shooter has a weakly dominant eye this can alter the eye-barrel relationship. For most shooters the effect becomes more apparent on longer shots. For many of our students, shooting with both eyes open is very ineffective. There are some easy remedies for eye-dominance troubles that I will cover soon.

Interestingly, eye dominance has different tendencies for males and females and for young and old. Most adult males tend to have the same dominant hand and dominant eye. However, a high percentage of adult females are cross-dominant, when the dominant eye and hand are opposite. I have a theory that this is because women tend to tap into both sides of the brain more freely than men do. I have no evidence to prove this, just a hunch. Young males in their teens can frequently switch eye dominance as they grow; their true eye dominance will often establish itself as they reach adulthood. As we grow older our eye dominance may weaken over time. This is especially true of people who tend to strain their eyes during a long day of work. This is also very common in people with a weakly dominant eye. I have seen many students' eye dominance change from one day to the next. Often the source of this is a long drive up from the city or a night of catching up on some reading.

There are numerous easy tests to determine what your dominant eye is. The most basic one is the "circle test." Make an OK sign by touching the tip of the thumb and pointer finger with the hand that holds the forend of the gun. Next, hold out this hand with both eyes wide open and look through the circle to an object on the wall. If you blink each eye, one after the other, you will notice that the object disappears when one of the eyes is closed. If you close your left eye and can still see the object on the wall your right eye is most likely dominant. This tells you that the right eye is peering though the circle even when both eyes are open.

I use the pointer-finger test in my classes. I have my students point with their forefinger at my nose from about fifteen feet away. As they hold out their hand and point with both eyes open, they see how the pointer finger lines up with the eyes. For someone who is strongly right-eye dominant the finger will line up directly with the right eye. I can tell if someone has a weakly dominant eye if the finger leans toward one eye but does not directly line up with either. You can also tell if someone has central vision with this test. I have seen many shooters test right- or left-eye dominant with the circle test, and then appear to have central vision during the pointer-finger test. So the pointer-finger test can give you more information than the circle test.

As I stated before, you should shoot with both eyes open if possible. But this is a workable option only if you have a strongly dominant eye on the same side of the shoulder you shoot from. What can you do if this is not the case? There are a number of options worth trying.

First, close your left eye as you complete the gun mount. This will allow the right eye to line up directly with the gun barrel and the target (assuming, again, that you are shooting off of the right shoulder). Be sure to close the eye at the correct moment. Many shooters close the left eye too soon. If you leave both eyes open during the beginning of the swing you can use binocular vision to track the speed, distance, and line of the bird. However, there is still time to squint the left eye before the stock touches the cheek and shoulder. When to shut the left eye often depends on the individual. Some prefer to squint the left eye early too avoid any confusion with seeing the tip of the gun barrel. Some shooters squint just before they pull the trigger. This squint will block out

(Top left) The pointer figure is lining up perfectly with the left eye. The left eye is clearly dominant. (Top right) This shooter appears to have central vision or not one overly powerful dominant eye. (Bottom) This shooter is clearly looking through the circle with the right eye.

the left eye from interfering with your aim and the right eye can line up perfectly with the target.

Another option is to block out the left eye by putting a small piece of tape on the shooting glasses. You can also use a lip balm to smudge out a small area on your glasses. Blocking out the correct area on the shooting glasses is essential, and this is best done by a professional coach. Many times this technique will help new shooters develop a proper gun mount even if they don't have any eye-dominance problem. The tape allows the eye and barrel to align without complicating the sight picture. This can really help a new shooter to develop a mount correctly. There are some problems with blocking out an eye and it may not work for someone who has an extremely cross-dominant eye. In that case the

In the ready the shooter can use both eyes.

dominant eye will try to look around the tape, which can cause problems during the swing and gun mount. The head will often twist and drop so the eye can peer around the tape. In such a situation, I recommend seeing a professional coach to help find a solution.

The shooter who is extremely cross-dominant is often advised to switch and shoot off of the other shoulder. This can be hard to do for some, but with a little practice it can really pay off in the long run. A new shooter who has no muscle memory can sometimes breeze right into this. I'm naturally right-handed, but I have a left master eye. I did switch and learn to shoot off of my left shoulder. It was a fairly smooth transition and a great learning experience. Being naturally right-handed and shooting off of the left

Once the gun is fully mounted, the tape, when properly placed, should block out the off eye.

shoulder put my true pointing hand on the forend of the gun. Right from the start I was able to point out the targets very effectively because my right hand was leading my swing. There are many positives that can come of switching shoulders to line up with the dominant eye. Again, I would advise you to do this under the supervision of a qualified shooting professional.

Eye dominance can be a tricky variable, especially during the gunfitting process. Before having a proper fitting you should have any eye-dominance issues resolved completely. Often, excessive cast is mistakenly bent into a stock to compensate for eye-dominance problems. Once the problem is solved by closing an eye or by another means, a shooter is left with a stock that has too much cast built into it.

Again, shooting with both eyes open is an advantage only if the dominant eye is strong enough and it matches up with the shoulder you shoot off of. I know many shooters who close the left eye just before completing their gun mount. Most do it so instinctively that they believe they are shooting with both eyes open. I have asked many students why they are closing an eye as they pull the trigger. Most replied, "I didn't know that I was closing an eye." This means that they have such unwavering attention on the target that even when they are shutting one eye they remain completely focused on the bird. Be sure that you are completely certain of how your eye dominance affects your overall shooting performance and style before you make any alterations to your stock.

CHAPTER
T W O

The Sight Picture and Forward Allowance

Focusing on the Bird

For many hunters nothing beats a crisp autumn afternoon of steady dog work and birds holding tight. It's a good day when you rise to the challenge and reward the efforts of your four-legged hunting partner by shooting straight. When you're done, a brace of birds rests on the tailgate and you're enjoying a drink straight from the flask. You can recall every bird as it took to the air and your shooting was like something out of a dream sequence. These memorable days linger all year until the next hunting season begins.

Having the right sight picture can make all the difference in the world. Your concentration and focus are so sharp that the target seems to be flying like a blimp. What exactly should you see when you pull the trigger? Your focus should be intensely on the target or even a specific part of the target, such as the leading edge. As you fully mount the gun the barrels can easily distract you. So at the moment you are going to pull the trigger you need

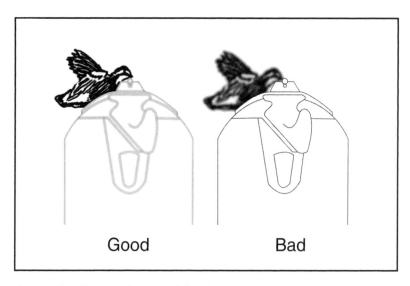

The gun should appear in our peripheral vision, but the focus should be keenly on the bird.

to focus hard on the bird. Look for the white ring on the neck of a pheasant, or focus only on the head of a duck as it passes over the blind. The best shotgunners can focus on the bird without being distracted by the barrels or a backdrop of trees and sky.

What about forward allowance or leading the bird when you shoot? There is no disputing the fact that you need to shoot ahead of certain birds. I've been asked this question countless times. "How much should I lead a bird?" The clay shooters are always trying to calculate how much lead is needed for a particular presentation. This crossing shot needs four feet or that quartering needs only six inches. The problem with this is that most shooters perceive things differently. Six inches for one person may seem like two feet for another.

In the field the wingshooter simply cannot figure out all the different angles and leads needed to shoot birds flying in the wild. The wingshooter also doesn't have time to sit and ponder the distance, speed, and angle of the bird. The field shot needs to instinctively react to a bird in flight and develop the correct lead naturally. The swing and mount of a field shooter should be designed to instinctively create the correct lead.

The wingshooter should be aware of lead, but should not try to measure it. Robert Churchill believed all wingshooters should "dismiss all ideas of calculated allowances."[4] The best field shots are aware of leading the bird, but do not try to measure how far ahead the muzzle is just before pulling the trigger. The act of "picturing" your lead without being distracted by the barrels is a product of visual concentration. A long and slow crossing shot might require a different picture than a close, fast one. However, your swing and concentration on the flight of the bird should help to naturally create the correct lead.

There are a number of methods to build or create lead. There is the swing-through method. Also there is maintained lead, pull away, and snap shooting. Some of these techniques are better for the wingshooter than others.

"Snap," or "spot" shooting is mostly used on upland game in tight cover. The snap shooter pokes the gun to a spot in hopes of connecting with the target rather than swinging along the flight path of the bird. This can work at close range and in thick cover where the shooting is cramped. Many New England grouse hunters spot shoot successfully, but this technique's effectiveness is very limited. Spot shooting has no real swing and follow-through to it. The gun typically comes to a stop once the shot is fired. This isn't something that would work well on medium- to long-range birds where follow-through is necessary.

In maintained, or sustained lead, the shooter holds the barrels a predetermined distance ahead of the bird during the swing and mount. Maintained lead is mostly used on clay targets where you can set up properly to be ahead of the bird from the get-go. This system requires a predetermined and calculated lead. This obviously does not suit the walk-up shooter when the birds flush and fly unpredictably. It can be used on pass shooting, but as a general rule sustained lead is not ideally suited for game shooting.

The swing-through method is a technique that is frequently used by wingshooters. Being able to overtake the bird by swinging along its flight path seems to work best when shooting game. In the field birds are unpredictable. Because of this you are often forced to play a game of catch-up. For this reason the swing-through method tends to work the best in the field.

The skilled wingshooter uses the pace of the bird to help swing ahead correctly. On a fast, close-range target, you must swing the gun ahead quickly so the lead is developed easily. On these targets the lead is almost effortless to develop, assuming the swing and mount are correct. When shooting at long-range birds, they seem to be moving slower, and you can easily miss behind these targets. Try not to be tempted into measuring the lead with the barrels. Use the swing of the body and gun to develop lead and take the shot in one smooth movement.

Churchill believed that you can naturally develop the correct lead by focusing intensely on the bird while using the body and footwork to swing the gun in one smooth motion. Churchill's theory called for lead to be developed unconsciously through unwavering concentration on the bird and by not seeing the barrels at all when shooting. This will allow the body and gun to swing ahead of the bird while the eyes remain locked on the bird. Churchill states, "The shooter should not be conscious of his gun-muzzle, the rib or sight. His eye or rather attention should be fully

There is a real difference between "picturing lead" and measuring lead. You will always perceive less lead if you can avoid focusing on the barrels.

occupied with the bird, and, if he holds his gun properly, he will hit whatever he is looking at."[5] Churchill also believed that the speed of the bird compels you to swing out ahead naturally. For a slow bird the swing-through will be minimal, but on fast birds the swing-through will naturally be greater.

Churchill's unconscious development of lead can be very effective on fast-moving, short- to medium-range birds. This unconscious approach to lead is ideal when walking up game and reactions need to be fast yet smooth. At the Orvis Shooting Schools our instructors recognize that unconsciously leading longer-range birds can be difficult. New shooters often have trouble on longer-range targets and often need to see generous lead pictures. Through practice and concentration a shooter will become more comfortable with the footwork, swing, and mount. As shooters improve, they develop a trust in the gun. They begin to see that the gun will shoot where the eyes are looking. Once this trust is created the correct lead picture becomes easier to develop. I often hear the misstatement that the instinctive method of shooting does not require lead. This is simply untrue. An instinctive shooter is aware of lead but does not measure it in terms of feet or inches.

Advice for Developing Lead

To instinctively swing through the bird the shooter must understand the subtleties of how and when to shoulder the gun. All too often the novice game shot will sling the gun up to the shoulder and then try to swing ahead of the bird. Don't mount the gun and then try to calculate the lead. The proper technique is to swing and mount the gun in one smooth action. The body should move with the gun as it is lifted to the shoulder and cheek. Most importantly, the swing-through should happen as the mount is completed. Try not to think about adding lead as an afterthought. You should swing ahead of the bird as you complete the mount. This will reduce any tendency to aim with the barrel and allows the body to pivot freely with the gun. As the birds bust, shooters often

Avoid mounting the gun to the shoulder then attempting to swing onto the bird. This is poor form that promotes "aiming" with the gun barrel.

Learn to swing the body with the gun to develop lead more effortlessly. The swing and mount should be one smooth action, with the gun coming into the shoulder and cheek only when the shot is ready to be taken.

want to rush the mount. But there is no sense mounting the gun unless you know what direction the birds are flying in. So swing the gun with the birds by pointing with the lead hand. As you do this the gun should naturally slide up to the shoulder and cheek. As you grow your swing and mount into one harmonious movement, developing the correct lead picture will feel much more natural.

This instinctive approach to developing lead is very effective when shooting birds at medium to close range. By focusing hard on the bird you are compelled to point and swing the gun on target. This intense focus allows you to shoot instinctively. This is when your reflexes take over and you forget about measuring a lead with the gun barrel. Remember that this is much easier to do with a gun that fits and shoots where your eyes are looking.

An important part of naturally developing lead is to learn to swing the body in harmony with the gun. This will help to develop muzzle speed, which is the key to swinging ahead of any bird. Follow-through should be a natural outflow of your swing and mount. If you move the gun with only the arms by slinging it across your chest, your swing will be very limited. When you pivot your body with the gun, you are less likely to stop your swing after you fire. By pivoting your body with the gun, your swing is elongated and the gun swings freely through the target.

PART TWO

The Elements of Gunfitting

CHAPTER
THREE

Taking Measure
of Your Gun

A fitted shotgun is designed to naturally point where the shooter is looking, and shooting a shotgun effectively is all about pointing, not aiming. This makes perfect sense because pointing requires no conscience alignment, which is very different from aiming. How can you shoot straight without aiming? Through gunfitting and by using the proper technique.

A well-fitting gun aligns effortlessly with the shooter's arms and eyes.

A fitted gun becomes a natural extension of the shooter's hands and eyes. As the target appears the shooter points the gun with the hands while the eyes focus on the flight path of the bird. As the gun is mounted to the cheek and shoulder the eyes remain locked on the target, so that the lead hand can continue tracking the bird. If the eyes lose focus on the target, usually through aiming with the barrels, then the hands will fail to stay the course. A miss is most likely a result of not clearly seeing what you are pointing at the moment you pull the trigger.

The master eye in shotgunning is a lot like the rear sight on a rifle. If the eye and the end of the gun are lined up then there is honestly no need to aim at a bird in flight. Simply lock onto the bird visually and point the gun where you're looking and the bird should fall end over end after the trigger is pulled. I'm sure this sounds a little oversimplified, and for some shots it may be. However, once you have the confidence that your gun aligns squarely with your eyes, easy shots become routine and difficult shots become easier.

The Try Gun

The tool of a professional gunfitter is the try gun. A try gun has a normal action and barrels, but the stock is fully adjustable. The gunfitter changes the dimensions of the try gun to fit the unique build and shape of the shooter. The goal of this manipulation of the try gun is to get the master eye and barrel in perfect alignment. These adjustments can be made quickly and easily so that

The try gun is the tool of the professional gunfitter.

A try gun can be easily adjusted to fit the build and style of an individual shooter.

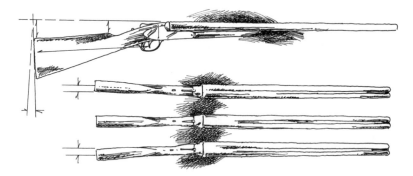

The elements of gunfit: Drop at comb (distance from the heel to the dashed line), angle of pitch (degree of the angle under the butt), length of pull (distance from the trigger to butt stock), and cast (overhead guns: top, "cast on"; center, neutral; bottom, "cast off").

the shooter can instantly see the results on the patterning board or on a clay target. The novice is usually amazed to see how much the point of impact can change on the patterning board with a few minor adjustments to the try gun during a fitting.

The primary elements of gunfit are length of pull, pitch, drop, and cast. I'll examine each of these individually. But keep in mind that these elements combined constitute a perfect gunfit, and each of these adjustments can have a direct effect on the other. For example, the pitch can affect the length of pull, and length can affect the drop. The elements of gunfit do not exist in a vacuum; they all relate and affect each other to some degree. When you align all of these refinements, the gun can be mounted effort-lessly and your shot pattern will blanket the bird without your having to look down the barrel. In this union of elements, you have, essentially, a perfect shotgun for an individual shooter.

Length of Pull

The length of the stock, including its inherent length of pull—the distance from the middle of the trigger to the middle of the butt stock—is always the most overexamined feature of how well a bird gun might fit. The prospective buyer dry mounts the gun, feeling it out and envisioning birds flushing wildly in all angles. But this tells you very little; it's just like taking a fly rod off the rack and wiggling it, which won't really tell you how it will perform when casting forty feet of line to a rising trout.

To be honest, the length of pull is only a small piece of the puzzle. The length of the stock is the most forgiving dimension when it comes to gunfit. For example, an ⅛-inch difference on the length will not affect the point of impact much, but a ⅛-inch change at the comb will have a tremendous effect on the elevation of your shot pattern.

I could comfortably shoot a gun with a 14¾-inch pistol grip up to a 15¼-inch straight grip. I don't mean to say that length of pull is not important, but you can comfortably tolerate a gun that is ¼ to ¾ of an inch too short. However, whichever length feels comfortable will affect where most of the other dimensions fall. So if a 14¾-inch length of pull mounts the best for you, then all the other gunfit dimensions will fall in line according to that length.

During a gunfitting I prefer to establish a comfortable length of pull for the shooter as a starting point. Once I figure this out, then I can start to examine some of the other dimensions with the try gun based on that stock length.

The length of pull determines where you place your cheek on the stock when the gun is fully mounted. Ideally, your cheek should fall slightly forward of the middle point between the drop at heel and drop at comb. So in essence, the head will be a touch closer to the comb than the heel of the stock. Length of pull in conjunction with the drops aligns the eye horizontally over the barrels, which establishes the elevation of your shot pattern.

What determines how long the stock should be? The old litmus test was to place the butt of the gun in the cradle of the arm while touching the trigger with the index finger. Unfortunately, this has nothing to do with figuring out length of pull. All that holding the gun that way will do is measure the distance from the trigger finger to the crook of your elbow.

How long the stock should be depends upon many factors: the overall length of your arms, the thickness or breadth of your

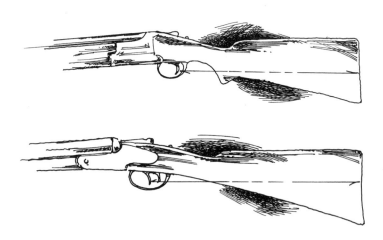

Above, length of pull is the distance from the trigger to the middle of the butt stock. *Below*, length of pull is measured from the first trigger on a double-trigger gun.

chest, length of your neck, and your gun-mounting style. Also taken under consideration is the placement of your lead hand on the forend, and your stance and foot positions. Finally, the grip style on the gun (pistol or straight) and single or double triggers can play a part in creating a stock length that best suits a shooter.

Physical features are obvious clues to determine stock dimensions. A long-armed person often points the gun out farther when swinging and mounting, so a stock should be made to accommodate that shooter's reach, whereas a barrel-chested, thicker man would certainly need the stock shorter than the long-armed, lanky fellow. A bulky-chested man needs a little more clearance from the butt stock to help slide the gun without interruption up to the cheek and shoulder. Also, if you have a shorter neck and a more upright mounting style, you would prefer a shorter stock length, as opposed to a long-necked shooter with a more lunging gun mount. I have a hunting partner who is five inches shorter than me, but his length of pull is longer than mine. This is because he has a long neck that he stretches forward as he mounts the gun. Because of this he can tolerate a much longer gun.

Fitting a gun for length is more art than science. Unfortunately there is no mathematical formula that calculates neck size, arm length, breadth of chest, and then factors in mounting style and spits out your perfect stock length. You determine your correct stock by learning to mount the gun consistently with proper form until the gun slides into the shoulder pocket and cheek without having to make any adjustments for its length.

Aside from physical features there are other factors that affect how long the stock should be. The placement of the lead hand on the forend of the gun can make it easier or harder to accommodate a par-

The correct length of pull comes about by mounting the gun consistently with proper form until the gun slides into the shoulder pocket and cheek without the shooter having to make any accommodations for its length.

ticular stock. If you cradle the forend closer to the action the gun will feel shorter. However, if you extend your lead hand out so that the arm is straighter, this will create the sensation of a longer stock. This can also be helpful during the hunting season because how much clothing you wear can affect how easy it is to mount the gun. The dove hunter might just wear a light shirt on opening day, but on a late-season quail hunt he might have on a sweater and an upland hunting jacket. The amount of clothing you wear can certainly have an effect on length of pull. I recommend that during a fitting you should try to wear whatever clothes you wear when hunting, if you can get that specific. For most shooters, however, the gun they buy will be shot on sporting clays in the heat of summer and at ducks in the frozen confines of the duck blind, so the clothes will always differ.

Some shooters will have a set of recoil pads made so they can change them out as needed. This can be a good idea, but remember that changing the stock length can change the elevation of your pattern. Also, changing the pads can be difficult and cumbersome.

But by changing the lead hand placement on the stock, you can make the gun feel longer or shorter without having to change the actual stock. Try this at home with your gun. Move the lead hand back and the gun will feel much shorter. Because you have more of a bend at the elbow to start with, you can extend the gun farther as you point at the bird. Also try holding the gun in the ready position with the arm extended so you are out farther on the forend. The gun will feel longer as you raise the gun and finish the mount. If your arm is already extended, you can't really reach out any farther. This creates less clearance for the stock as it is drawn out from under the armpit, so the stock feels longer to mount. These slight changes in your lead hand position can help accommodate the extra bulk of warm hunting clothes that, in effect, change your body's dimensions.

Your stance or foot placement in the ready position can also prescribe what length of pull suits you. The more you adopt a rifle stance and sling the gun across your body the longer the stock you can soak up. Of course, this is poor shooting form for shotgunning, as noted in the section on technique, but many hunters adopt the same stance and footwork for both their rifle and shotgun. To allow for a better gun mount in the shoulder pocket, take a slightly squarer stance than you would with a rifle. A squarer stance sets you correctly to swing the gun in any direction. If you pull your right foot too far back then you are likely to mount the gun on the biceps rather than in the shoulder pocket. Again, try to adopt as narrow a stance as possible without compromising balance. Next square up your stance and body slightly so that your lead foot, barrels, and midsection are all pointing in the general shooting direction. This will help you to avoid slinging the gun across your body, which can make the stock feel too short and uncomfortable to mount. (See the section on stance, pp. 16–22.)

Your gun's type of grip and triggers also warrant consideration when determining the length of pull. The difference between a pistol grip and a straight grip is usually about ¼ inch. This means that if you shoot a 14¼-inch pistol grip (over-under) then you could shoot a 14½-inch straight grip (over-under). If you prefer a pistol grip that is fine, just make sure you take that into consideration if you were fitted with a straight-gripped try gun. With a pistol grip the wrist and hand are held differently. In effect it shortens your reach a little on your grip hand, and that is the reason why a curved-gripped stock can be shorter. Note, however, that double triggers call for a longer stock than a single-trigger gun, and are thus often matched to a straight grip. A slightly longer stock creates the extra room needed to touch each trigger effortlessly.

What is the cause and effect of shooting a gun that is not the correct length? Well, the wrong length of pull can make it awfully hard to connect with a covey of quail as they bust from the brush. You should always shoot with a stock that is as lengthy as possible, as long as the length does not hamper your swing and gun mount. However, if the gun is too long this can cause you to mount the gun outside of the shoulder pocket. Have you ever gotten a bruise on the biceps after a day of shooting? This is most likely from a stock that is too long and it just can't fit correctly into the shoulder pocket. Also, a stock that is too long may cause the gun to pattern left for a right-handed shooter. This is because the

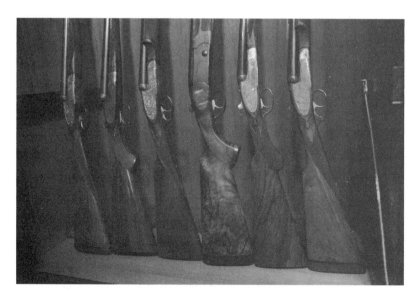

Triggers and grip styles can have a subtle effect on length of pull.

shooter cannot accommodate the stock as he slings the gun across his body, dragging the barrels slightly left of the target. More often that not, if a stock is too long this will cause the gun to shoot high. In the struggle to slide the stock up into the shoulder and cheek, the barrels tend to raise up to the target ahead of the stock, so as you complete the mount the shot sails higher than if the stock and barrels rose up together to meet the bird.

Shooting a gun with a stock that is too short, however, can cause some problems of its own. You can mount a gun that is a little too short, of course, but it is nearly impossible to fully mount one that is truly too long. A gun that is too short often produces more felt recoil, because the gun may not be fully seated against your shoulder when you pull the trigger. Also, a shooter with a gun that is too short tends to encroach across the barrels as the mount is finished; the shooter's head drops down and over to meet the stock, putting the dominant eye over the center line of the rib and causing the shot to go right. A miss to the right for a right-handed shooter is often misdiagnosed as too much cast. If the shooter is dropping his head down to meet the gun, then the stock is too short. Simply lengthening the stock to the proper pull will often cure a miss to the right.

One of the most common flaws that you experience in shooting a gun that is too short is that the stock tends to come up to your cheek and shoulder ahead of the barrels. This creates a see-saw effect during the gun mount. A short stock makes the hands work independently during the mount and the gun wobbles as you lift it. Another frequent problem is that the swing can be interrupted when shooting a short stock. This happens because the shooter has to pull the stock back to meet the shoulder. This

A stock that is too long will be difficult to fully mount. The result is often a miss high because the barrels come up ahead of the stock.

When mounting a stock that is too short, the cheek is often too forward on the stock, and the head is tilted over the comb.

pulling-back motion breaks the flow of the swing and mount. The benefit of shooting a longer stock is that it creates a more balanced gun.

When you establish the correct length of pull the hands tend to work together as you mount the gun. Figuring out the length of pull is best achieved through trial and error. This can be time consuming, and making continuous adjustments to the length of your gun isn't easy. It is best done under the watchful eye of a professional gunfitter with an adjustable try gun.

Pitch

The pitch of your gun is the angle of the butt stock compared to the barrels. If a gun is set up with a pitch of zero, the angle between the butt stock and the barrel is 90 degrees. However, if the butt stock is shaped so that the toe is cut back from the heel, this is considered positive pitch. Pitch in America is measured in degrees. So if the angle between the barrels and the stock is 89 degrees, this would be +1 degree of pitch. An 88-degree cut would be +2 degrees, 87 degrees would be +3 degrees, and so on. I would say that the average field gun ends up with +4 degrees of pitch. This means the butt stock in relation to the barrel forms an 86-degree angle.

Negative pitch is when the angle between the butt stock and the barrel exceeds 90 degrees. This would mean that the heel of the butt stock is cut back shorter than the toe. So 91 degrees would be −1 degree of pitch, 92 degrees of pitch would be −2 degrees, and so forth. For comfort reasons, negative pitch is much less common because the pronounced toe would point uncomfortably into the chest of most shooters.

The reason for adjusting the pitch of the butt stock is to reduce felt recoil on the shoulder and to help adjust the elevation of the shot. The primary goal when adjusting the pitch is to make sure that the angle of the butt stock matches the contour of the upper chest. This is to ensure that the recoil is evenly distributed throughout the shoulder and upper chest. For example, a barrel-chested man or a woman would certainly need more positive pitch than a slender, tall person. If the stock does not have enough positive pitch, the toe of the butt points into the upper chest and the heel does not even come in contact with the shoulder. For obvious reasons this can be a common occurrence in barrel-chested men and women. Not enough positive pitch means that the recoil is felt much more in the toe because the butt stock is not flush with the entire chest and shoulder. The brunt of the recoil is funneled through the toe into the upper chest as the shot is fired. This can be very uncomfortable especially after a full day of shooting.

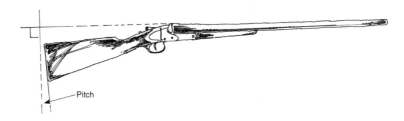

Measuring pitch by the angle of the butt in relation to the barrels.

Correctly adjusting pitch is very important to ensure a comfortable shooting gun. The proper pitch angle will allow the entire butt stock to be in contact with the shoulder and chest. If the contour of the shoulder and upper chest matches the pitch of the gun, then the recoil is evenly distributed throughout the entire butt. This will translate into a more comfortable shooting gun with less felt recoil.

Pitch is adjusted for comfort, but the angle of the butt can have an effect on the elevation of your shot pattern. The drops have a more direct effect on the elevation of your shot string. However, the angle of the butt stock can also contribute to how high or low your gun can shoot. For example, if you decrease the pitch, this will cause the gun to shoot higher. Likewise, if you increase the pitch, it will make the gun shoot lower. Imagine if you had a gun with an adjustable pitch. If you mounted this gun cleanly to your shoulder and then began to decrease the pitch, this would cause the barrels to move up slightly. As you increased the pitch the barrels would lower as you kept the butt stock flush with the upper chest and shoulder.

Some guns built exclusively for driven-bird shooting will have very little positive pitch, or even some negative pitch. This is because most of the shots are high incoming, so it pays to have the gun patterning high. Also, because of the nature of swinging and mounting the gun on a high incoming bird, a shooter can accommodate a very low pitch of say +1 or +2. Some stocks come fashioned with a negative pitch. Many trap guns will have a pitch of −1 or −2 degrees. Trap shooting has only rising targets so this pitch arrangement is an advantage, as the shooter will usually premount the gun to the shoulder and cheek making sure that the butt stock is comfortable in position. For most field guns, however, the pitch will range from +3 to +8 degrees depending on the build of the shooter.

The pitch and length of a gun have a direct link with each other. Adjusting the pitch should be built in to finding the correct length of pull. Many times a woman will show up for a lesson with a gun that was selected by a well-meaning husband. The husband's first move is usually to hack off some of the stock so that his wife can handle the gun. But the pitch of angle of the butt stock is almost never taken into consideration in such a customization. Simply shortening a gun from 14½ inches to 13¾ inches might be the right course of action, but if the gun still has a pitch of +3 degrees it will feel too long and will be uncomfortable to shoot. Whenever adjusting the length of pull, the pitch must always be taken into consideration. This will ensure that the gun will be comfortable to shoot, accurately pattern, and mount easily.

To measure the pitch of a gun, a fitter will use a special drop stick that can accurately read the angle of the butt stock in relation to the barrels. The drop stick looks something like a large protractor that measures pitch in degrees. If you don't have a drop stick that can measure pitch, you can figure it out simply with a ruler and a level floor or doorway. Begin by placing a small piece of tape on the rib at the 26-inch mark near the end of the barrels. Next, stand the gun so that the butt stock is flush with the floor and the receiver leans against the wall. Measure the distance between the 26-inch mark and the wall. A half inch will equal 1 degree of pitch. So if the distance between the gun barrel and the wall is 2 inches then the pitch is +4 degrees. If the distance is 2½ inches then the pitch would be +5 degrees. The math is easy enough, but you must

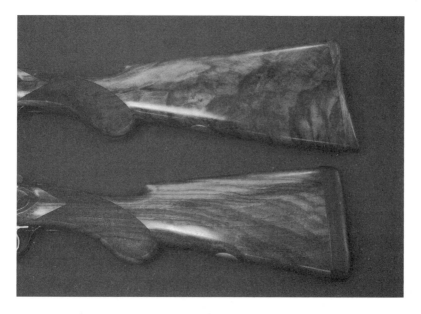

A pronounced toe can create an uncomfortable pitch angle. A butt stock with more rounded features can be more comfortable to shoot.

be consistent and measure at the 26-inch mark. If you were to measure the distance at the end of the barrel and that gun had, say, 30-inch barrels, then this would certainly skew things.

Drop

Drop (or "bend," as the English call it) is the distance from the rib to the top line of the stock. Drop is composed of two measurements: the drop at comb and the drop at heel. These two dimensions chiefly determine the elevation of the eye as it sights down the rib. The place where the cheek comes to rest between the comb and heel is sometimes referred to as "drop at face." There is no practical need to measure drop at face when fitting a shooter. However, this term is often used to describe the point where the cheek rests on the stock.

Drop at comb, and to a lesser extent drop at heel, determines how high or how low your gun will shoot. The combination of these two measurements dictates the height of the dominant eye in relation to the rib. If you could peer down the muzzle of your gun in the mounted position, you would see how your eye, particularly the pupil, sits over the rib. The height of the eye over the barrel will determine how high or low your gun will pattern. If your gun has too much drop, the eye will be looking into the back of the receiver. If you have too little drop, then the eye rests well above the rib and your gun will shoot high. Ideally the master eye aligns directly down the sight line of the barrels. There is some room for individual preference with your drop to create the optimum pattern for your bird gun.

The most accepted pattern for field shooting is about 60:40. On the patterning board this would translate into a pattern that is slightly above center of the target; 60 percent of the pellets will blanket over the bird and 40 percent hit below. This is considered the classic pattern for the upland hunter. Because birds rise as they

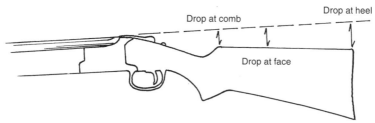

Drop at comb and heel.

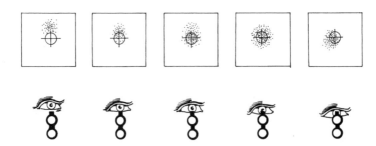

This is a rough idea of how a gun would pattern depending on how high the eye rests over the barrels. For best results, shoot at the patterning plate.

flush from cover, using a gun that shoots a touch high is an advantage. This also allows you to clearly see what you are shooting at without having to cover up the target with the barrels as some bird hunters claim to do. Hitting a bird on the wing can be terribly difficult if you can't see what you're shooting at.

The trap shooter or driven-bird shooter might prefer a higher pattern, and a skeet or sporting clay shooter might prefer lower. The type of pattern that best suits you is a personal choice. Some prefer a relative falter pattern of say fifty-fifty when pass shooting ducks or shooting sporting clays. However, other shooters feel more comfortable with a higher pattern when upland hunting quail, pheasants, or grouse. A classic upland pattern has a point of impact that is about 60 percent high, and this can be a nice help on rising game. Who doesn't want a little advantage in the field?

Most field gunners will have a drop at comb that is between $1\frac{1}{4}$ inches to $1\frac{5}{8}$ inches, and a drop at heel somewhere between $2\frac{1}{8}$ inches to $2\frac{5}{8}$ inches. Anyone needing drops that do not fall within that range is very rare. Also, note that there should be no more than a 1-inch difference between drop at comb and drop at

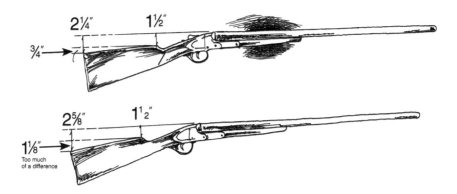

If possible it is best to have no more than ¾ of an inch difference between the drop and comb and heel. This will create less felt recoil for the shooter.

heel. If possible, have no more than a ¾-inch difference between the drop at comb and heel. This is particularly true of a female shooter and slender men with higher cheekbones. There are practical reasons to strive for a less than a 1-inch differential between drop at comb and drop at heel. For one, as the gap between the comb and heel increases, it can create more muzzle flip, or jump, when the gun is fired. This translates into more felt recoil, especially on the cheek. Excessive drop at heel, more than 1-inch from the comb, will pull the end of the stock well below the plane of the barrels. This will create an uncomfortable and clumsy-feeling gun, especially when fired. This becomes increasingly noticeable on doubles. Many older field guns have this type of drop configuration. The gun jumps so much after the first shot that the shooter has trouble recovering and locking onto the next bird in the covey. A ¾-inch differential creates a comfortable, balanced gun that points and shoots more accurately.

The average field stock is typically around 1½ inches at the comb and 2¼ inches at the heel for men. The average female shooter drops out around 1⅜ inches at the comb and 2⅛ inches at the heel. I am, of course, speaking for Mr. and Ms. Average. What drops actually work depend on the unique build and style of the shooter.

Drop at Comb

As explained earlier, drop at comb is the distance from the comb on the top of the stock to the rib on the barrel. This dimension has the most direct effect on how high or how low your gun will pattern. Even a slight change of ⅛ of an inch here will have a tremendous effect on the elevation of your pattern. The cheek comes to rest on the stock about 2 inches behind the drop at comb. This means that raising or lowering the comb will directly affect the height of the eye in relation to the barrels. So a ⅛-inch adjustment at the comb will have a much more profound effect on elevation of the eye than a ⅛-inch movement at the heel. This is not to say that drop at heel will not affect the elevation of your shot—it will. But drop at comb has a more direct effect on how high or low your gun will shoot. Depending on the length of the stock, it would take a significant movement at the heel to affect the eye in relation to the barrel. Even if someone is fitted with a longer stock, the shooter's cheek must still come to rest slightly behind the drop at comb, which means that the drop at comb truly controls the elevation of the gun's pattern.

Most shooters fall somewhere in between 1¼ inches to 1⅝ inches at the comb. A slight woman with high cheekbones may need only 1¼ inches, whereas a tall, burly man with a fuller face may need 1⅝ inch at the comb. The male shooter of average build typically is around 1½ inches at the comb. The standard off-the-rack shotgun is usually built with 1½ inches of drop in the comb, because such guns are mass-produced to suit the average bird hunter.

What are the primary factors that dictate what the drop at comb should be? The most apparent factor is the distance from the eye (specifically the iris) to the underbelly of the cheekbone. Other factors that contribute to how much drop is needed at the comb can be the fullness of the face and cheeks and the gun-mounting style.

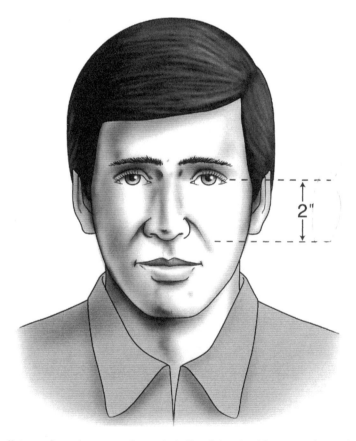

The distance from the eye to the underbelly of the cheekbone can determine how much drop at comb a shooter may need. Other factors can be fullness of face and cheeks, along with gun-mounting style.

Someone with high cheekbones and a thin build would certainly have less distance between the center of the eye and the underpart of the cheekbone. This calls for less drop at the comb to help the eye sight correctly down the barrel. Also, the fullness of the cheeks and facial structure can affect how much drop is needed. Someone who is heavyset with a full, round face may need more than average drop. Some extra jowl can be helpful in cushioning recoil, but it can also create more space between the eye and cheekbone. Facial structure in general can dictate how much drop will be needed. A short face with high cheekbones would need less drop, and a long face would need more.

A shooter's gun-mounting style can also have an effect on drop. Someone with an aggressive, firm gun mount may need less drop than someone who lightly touches the gun to the cheek. How the gun comes into contact with the cheek can vary depending on the shooter. An older gun or a new shotgun can affect the development of your mounting style. Many times a bird hunter will learn to shoot with Granddad's old double, which for the most part does not fit well. The gun is a treasured keepsake, but many of these older American side-by-sides have a good bit of drop in them. By shooting a gun with too much drop the shooter learns to compensate by keeping the head up and not aggressively mounting the gun to the cheek. This is poor form, but with some practice the shooter learns to knock down a bird or two with it. The reason a shooter does not want to fully mount a gun with too much drop is that the master eye will be looking into the back of the receiver rather than down the rib. This is so much drop that the eye is blocked from sighting down the rib correctly.

The gun mount can create a tricky situation when properly fitting a shotgun. A shooter who has a very inconsistent or poor gun mount should not be fitted. I firmly believe that for a gunfitting to be absolutely accurate the shooter must have a consistent and repeatable gun mount. This ensures that the eye is correctly aligning with the barrel every time the gun is fully mounted. Most game shooters want the center portion of the eye to be slightly above the rib when the gun is perfectly mounted. This allows the shooter to see the bird clearly while the eye sights down the barrel.

Drop at Heel

Drop at heel is the distance from the plane of the rib to the heel on the stock. Drop at heel affects how high the gun will shoot, but it also establishes where the butt of the gun will come to rest on the shoulder. Ideally, the heel of the gun should line up very near the top of the shoulder when the gun is fully mounted. There is a little room for variation here. Depending on the shooter, some people can be comfortable with the butt of the gun coming to rest slightly below the top of the shoulder.

Pitch helps the butt of the gun come into full contact with the slope of the upper chest. Drop at heel then helps to ensure that the top line of the gun lies flush with the top of the shoulder. A gun with too much drop at heel would place the butt of the gun well below the top line of the shoulder and onto the chest. This would be a difficult gun to mount effectively. Most often a shooter has to drop the head down to meet the stock of a gun with too much drop at heel. Head movement is a leading cause of missed shots for beginner and expert alike. Conversely, too little drop at heel would place the top of the stock above the shoulder. This can create a gun that is

A comfortable drop at heel will put the butt of the stock on the upper chest. The heel should not be so high that the heel is above the shoulder blade. Notice here that the butt of the gun fits snugly into the shoulder pocket.

very uncomfortable to shoot because the toe would funnel the brunt of the recoil into the top of the collarbone or upper chest.

The drop at heel can be affected by the distance from the top of the shoulder to the rib or top of the barrel. The slope of a shooter's shoulders, length of the neck, and gun-mounting style can also dictate how much drop is needed at the heel. A long-necked shooter who holds the head very erect when mounting the gun will benefit from more drop at heel. A short-necked, stout shooter may need less drop at heel to fit the stock correctly into the shoulder pocket. However, the X factor is the style of the gun mount. That same long-necked shooter who leans into the shoot and lunges the head forward would most likely need less drop at heel than if the head remained erect during the gun mount.

Most shooters will have a drop at heel that ranges from 2 inches to $2\frac{5}{8}$ inches. The vast majority tend to fall in at $2\frac{1}{4}$, $2\frac{3}{8}$, or $2\frac{1}{2}$ inches at the heel. Physical features can dictate how a gun may fit, but how you mount the gun certainly affects the overall dimensions that suit you best. Gunfit is a blend of science and art. The science is in the geometry, but your swing and gun mount are the art.

Cast

Cast is the degree to which the stock is bent right or left of the rib or barrels. This allows the eye to be centered horizontally down the rib without having to cant the head over the stock. If drop is used to control the elevation then think of cast as your windage.

A try gun has an adjustable knuckle that can easily create cast in the stock.

Drop and cast are the most important elements in fitting a stock, because they have the most direct effect on the accuracy of your shot pattern. A $\frac{1}{8}$-inch adjustment in the cast or drop can dramatically affect the eye-barrel relationship. Whereas a $\frac{1}{8}$-inch adjustment in the length of pull would most likely go unnoticed and not greatly affect the eye-barrel relationship. Drop and cast adjustments are precise and directly contribute to making sure that your bird gun is pointing and shooting where your eyes are looking.

The average shooter will typically need about $\frac{1}{8}$ to $\frac{1}{4}$ of an inch of cast. Some shooters may need as much as $\frac{3}{8}$ to $\frac{1}{2}$ inch of cast bent into the stock, but this is less common. "Cast off" is used to describe the stock being angled slightly to the right. "Cast on" is the term used when the stock is angled slightly to the left. Obviously, right-handed shooters prefer cast off, and left-handed shooters favor cast on.

With the proper cast, the shooter can mount the gun without having to push the head and nose aggressively into the stock. It allows the eye to horizontally line up with the end of the barrel much more easily. Cast is primarily measured at the heel and toe. Some stock makers and fitters might also measure the cast at face as well. Although cast is primarily measured at the heel, achieving cast at the toe and face is what's most important. Most shooters only need relief at the drop face for the eye, and then at the toe for the slope of the shoulder pocket. If the heel of the stock is cast too much, it may force the butt of the gun to land outside of the shoulder pocket.

Depending on the contours of the shoulder and chest some shooters will benefit from a touch more cast at the toe than at the heel. A broad-chested man with sloping shoulders or a busty woman could certainly benefit from cast built into the toe. This will help place the butt sole correctly along the shoulder pocket and upper chest. If ⅛ inch of cast was needed at the heel, then ³⁄₁₆ or ¼ inch could sometimes be prescribed at the toe.

Cast should be doled out sparingly, though, especially on over-under models. Excessive cast, particularly at the heel, can be troublesome. Because the more the cast is off or on, the more out

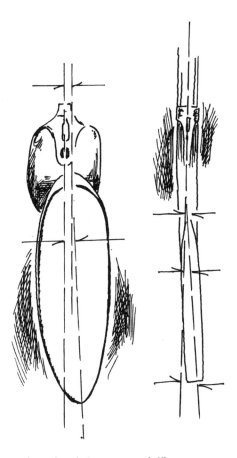

Rear view of cast and overhead view on cast (off).

of alignment the end of the stock will be with the barrels. The farther the butt stock is from the center of the rib, the greater the
negative recoil effect. Excessive recoil caused by too much cast
can actually pull the barrels in the opposite direction, despite the
fact that the eye is centered over the rib. As an example, too much
cast off can cause the gun to shoot more to the left, which is what
cast off is trying to correct for a right-handed shooter. This is less
common with side-by-sides because the cast may actually center
the butt of the stock with the right barrel when fired. (This assumes,
of course, that it is cast off for a right-handed shooter and the
right barrel is being fired first.) In some cases cast will place the

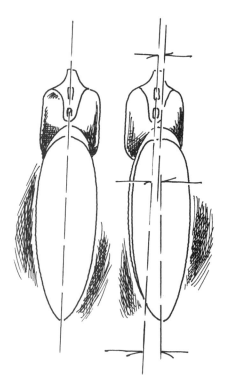

Sometimes a shooter can benefit from a little more cast at the
toe. This can help the butt of
the gun fit into the slope of the
shoulder pocket.

right barrel and the heel of the stock in nearly perfect alignment, creating less felt recoil and a pleasant shooting gun. Cast can help to center your shot pattern left to right, but use only enough to center the eye on the rib and no more.

A shooter who needs excessive cast might consider having a "scooped" stock or a swept-face stock made. A scooped stock has some wood shaved away on the comb at the exact spot where the cheek is mounted on the gun. This creates a little space for the head so that the eye can center on the rib without having to excessively bend the stock out of line with the barrels. A swept-face stock works on the same concept, with the "sweep blended into the stock in a long, smooth, concave curve." A swept-face stock is often carved into the desired shape from a solid block of wood rather than bent into position with oil or steam. One concern with a stock that has been scooped is that it can hurt the resale value of the gun. Also, a scooped-out stock does not have the sleek lines that are typically associated with a fine shotgun and it personalizes the gun somewhat. However, a great deal of cast can be created in either style and without the side effects of the excess recoil caused by the heel being out of line with the plane of the barrels.

How much cast is needed can be affected by the slope of the shoulders, shape of the face (round and full or long and thin), and how wide apart or narrow the eyes sit. The general shape of the face can be a telltale indication for how much cast will be needed. A person with a full, round face generally needs more cast than a person with a long, thinner face. However, facial structure is just a generalization. The most telling factor that contributes to a need for cast is the set of the eyes. The distance between the eyes truly affects the need for cast. I have fitted large, full-faced men who needed very little cast because their eyes were set very far apart. I have also doled out a ⅜-inch cast for thin-faced shooter whose eyes were set rather close together.

If the gun is cast correctly the sole of the butt will match the slope of the shoulders. Someone with a full chest and rounded shoulders might need more cast, especially at the toe, so that the gun can be comfortably mounted in the shoulder pocket. A shooter with very narrow, square shoulders might not need as much cast, particularly at the toe. The contour of the upper chest

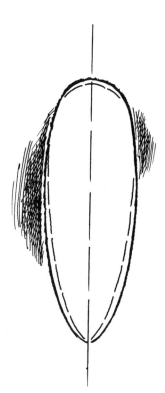

The thickness of the stock, particularly around the comb, is a variable worth considering when dealing with cast.

and shoulders must be taken into consideration when adjusting the cast at heel and toe.

The thickness of the stock, particularly around the comb, is a variable worth considering when dealing with cast. You might often hear that a thick-faced man should have a thin comb design, and that a thin-faced shooter should have a thick comb. The truth of it is that the thickness of the comb is an individual choice. Some thick-faced shooters do not like the feel of a dainty, little thin-stock comb. It just doesn't feel right to them. I have a thin face, and I prefer a thinner comb design, especially on my field gun. A gun with a thick comb feels cumbersome to me. However, I wouldn't say that the thickness of the comb is irrelevant when dealing with cast. You should understand that ⅛ inch of cast is not

Dogs are often bewildered by bad shots—they expect to find a bird after they hear the gun. So gunfit does play a role in your relationship with your dogs.

the same for each stock. A gun that is bent ⅛ of an inch but has a thick comb is certainly not the same as a ⅛-inch of cast on a stock that is very thin. Also, if you are fitted with a try gun that has a thin comb and you purchase a gun that has a thicker comb you most likely will need more cast in your new gun. I have seen this many times. A shooter is fitted with a thin-combed .20-gauge try gun. Then with the dimensions from that fitting the shooter purchases a thicker-comb .12 gauge. The ⅛ of an inch that was prescribed with the thin-combed try gun is not nearly enough for the new, bulkier .12 gauge. So you need to be sure that you're talking about apples for apples and not apples for oranges when deciding on comb thickness and cast.

There are so many variables to properly fitting a shotgun that it can seem like an overwhelming endeavor. The results, however, can improve your shooting tremendously and create a gun that you'll treasure until the time comes to hang it up over the fireplace. The guidance of a professional gunfitter can ease the process and help to ensure that you're confident with stock dimensions that are best for you. If you're serious about wing-shooting then the quest for the ideal bird gun begins with gunfit.

CHAPTER
F O U R

The Dimensions
of Gunfit

Checking and Measuring
the Fit of a Gun

Many bird hunters simply don't have access to a professional gunfitter and a try gun. Finding a professional gunfitter can be problematic, and if you track one down he usually resides two airline hubs away. So if you're on your own, here are some steps you can take to ensure that your bird gun does fit reasonably well.

A gunfitter will use mainly a drop stick to quickly figure out the cast, drop, and pitch. Armed with a tape measure and a flat table you can figure the dimensions of your favorite shotgun in no time.

Let's begin with the easiest measure: length of pull. Simply measure the distance from the trigger to the center of the butt stock. The average off-the-rack gun will be anywhere from 14¼ to 14¾ inches long. How do you know if the gun is too long or short? If the stock is too long you would notice this pretty quickly. If the heel routinely hangs up on the upper chest, making it difficult to raise the gun to the cheek and shoulder pocket, then the stock is most likely too long for you. A gun that is too short will be easier to mount, but

A gunfitter will use mainly a drop stick to quickly figure out the cast, drop, and pitch. Armed with a tape measure and a flat table you can figure the dimensions of your favorite shotgun in no time.

this can have noticeable problems also. For example, if you have to pull the butt back into the shoulder at the finish of the gun mount then the stock is probably too short. A stock that is the proper length should slide up to the shoulder along the contours of the upper chest. If there is excess space between you and the butt of the gun the recoil should be quite noticeable. To avoid being kicked many shooters will pull the gun back into the shoulder pocket at the finish of the mount. Also, a gun that is too short tends to swing poorly because of this pulling-back motion. You want the gun to swing out to the bird, and the shoulder to meet the stock effortlessly. If you have to pull the gun back and check your swing, the result is often a miss.

You can easily see when a stock is too short. There should be around 2 inches of space between your cheek and the thumb on your grip hand when the gun is fully mounted. Many shooters look as if they're going to punch themselves in the face with the grip hand when shooting a stock that is excessively short. You can check the spacing of your grip hand and cheek with a video camera. You can also peek into a mirror through the corner of your eye to see the profile of your gun mount. If a gun is too short, a quick fix may be a slip-on recoil pad. Most add around ½ inch, and in some cases this can really make the gun more comfortable to shoot.

The length of your stock is easier to critique. Figuring out if the drops, cast, and pitch are right for you can be more difficult to discern. As stated before, slight adjustments in the eye-barrel relationship have a tremendous effect on your shot pattern. So as you sight down the barrel of your gun it can be hard to judge with the naked eye that you need a ⅛-inch more drop at comb or a ⅛-inch cast off. Keep this in mind, but there are some ways of detecting flaws in cast, drop, and pitch.

To measure the drops on your gun, place it upside down on a level table. Make sure that the rib rests flat and the bead hangs off the end of the table. Next, take a ruler and measure the distance from the comb to the table. This will give the drop at comb. Measure the distance from the heel to the table, and this will tell you the drop at heel. The average drop at comb on a field gun is around 1½ inches. The average drop at heel is between 2¼ and 2½ inches. These dimensions can vary greatly depending on the model and vintage of the shotgun.

The drop mostly controls the eye's height in relation to the rib and the elevation of your shot pattern. To figure out if your drops suit you, try a few do-it-yourself tests.

First, mount the gun by keeping focus on an object on the wall and avoid aiming with the bead. Close the off eye and peer down the barrel. If you see the entire rib clearly then your gun eye is resting well above the sight line of the barrels. This gun will most likely pattern high. If you see only the bead and no rib then the gun will pattern flat. This means that the pattern is centered 50 percent high and 50 percent low of the target. This is OK for some clay shooting, but most bird hunters prefer a slightly higher shot pattern. If you can't see the bead at all you're probably looking into the back of the receiver. If the stock has excessive drop, the gun will pattern low. This gun might also pattern to the left because the right eye cannot focus down the barrel and the left eye takes over (assuming that your right eye is dominant and you shoot off of the right shoulder with both eyes open). The drop is presumably suitable if the master eye can see the bead and a bit of rib. This often creates a pattern that is a touch high, which is ideal for game shooting.

If the stock does not have enough drop, some of the wood can be sanded away so that the eye rests lower in relation to the rib. Anytime you put sandpaper to a fine piece of walnut you should do so only under the guidance of a qualified gunsmith. I certainly understand the dynamics of a try gun and gunfit, but I don't trust

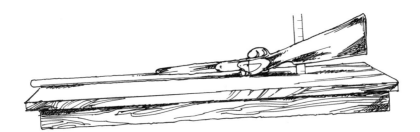

You can easily measure the drops with a ruler.

This stock has too much drop for this shooter. This gun will likely pattern low and left.

This gun does not have enough drop. This gun will mostly pattern too high for most shooters.

myself enough to handle stock work on my own guns—that is best left to a professional gunsmith. Some autoloaders with synthetic stocks come with shims that can adjust drop. These are relatively easy to fit and can help alleviate the problems with drop. In some cases, simply adding length can help. The increased length, if needed, will draw the face farther back from the comb, thereby lowering the eye over the barrel. This works only if the shooter can handle the extra length, and the slope of the stock provides enough drop for the eye. Obviously, this would not work on a parallel comb or a Monte Carlo-style stock.

If a stock has too much drop then the eye needs to be raised so that the shooter can sight correctly down the barrel. This is common with women and children who have higher cheekbones. Even with the stock shortened on a man's gun that is used by a woman or young person, the gun still has way too much drop, especially at the comb. Padding on the stock with some moleskin or some other type of soft material is a temporary fix. This is not my favorite option, but in a jam it can work. Some manufacturers make pads that lie over the comb to raise the eye and they claim this reduces felt recoil. These types of pads can be found relatively easily and can be helpful. They come in different thicknesses with adjustments from $\frac{1}{8}$ to $\frac{1}{2}$ inch. The best ones require no messy adhesives that can mar your stock. I prefer the type that fits easily on the top of the comb and isn't too bulky. Some pads are very thick and fit all the way around the stock. These can adversely affect cast. Often you have fixed one problem only to create another with a bulky wraparound pad.

As discussed in chapter 2, the pitch of your gun can be figured out with a tape measure and some simple math. As a shooter, you must understand that the pitch can affect the pattern of your shotgun. Also, if the toe of the gun is felt digging into the upper chest, then you most likely need the pitch adjusted. The goal is to have the butt stock conform to the slope of the upper chest. If either the heel or toe is not touching the upper chest then the pitch is mostly off a little. The correct pitch will create a more comfortable gun with less left recoil on the shoulder.

A surefire way to see if a stock suits you is to pattern the gun. By patterning your gun, the results can be seen clearly. Also by doing this there is no need to peek down the barrel to see if the eye lines up with the bead. The proof will be on the patterning board.

A patterning board is a whitewashed iron plate with a target painted in the center. The patterning plates Orvis uses are rounded slightly, somewhat like the exterior of a half barrel, to help prevent the pellets from bouncing back at the shooter. Many clay ranges have a station with a patterning board. If your local shooting club does not have one you can build a makeshift patterning plate with construction paper, a wood frame, and some hay bales. Make sure that you are shooting up to the target slightly, as shooting at a target below eye level is awkward and unnatural. Most shots taken in the field are rising, so place the patterning plate a foot or two above eye level.

Robert Churchill developed a system for interpreting the results of patterning a shotgun. His method requires you to be exactly sixteen yards from the patterning board. No less, no more. Churchill's approach also presumes that "the eye is thirty-six inches from the gun muzzle, [and] that the gun shoots with true elevation and the two barrels are in the same line."[6] If all this is

The proof will be on the patterning board.

not perfect, don't worry. You can still get a good read on the fit of your gun by patterning it.

Paint a bull's-eye in the center of your patterning plate about an inch in diameter. To ensure a true reading on the fit of your stock be sure not to aim the gun like a rifle during this exercise. You could mold yourself to any stock given the time to adjust your mount and take aim.

To avoid aiming, begin from a correct ready position. Then raise the gun to the shoulder and cheek without adjusting the head to accommodate the stock. Avoid snapping the gun up to the shoulder. Simply focus on the bull's-eye as if it were a flushing bird, and make a smooth gun mount, trying not to see the end of the barrel. I recommend during a fitting to try to mount the gun as slowly as possible, up to the point that you're not deliberately aiming.

Take three shots per sheet of paper or whitewashing. If your gun mounts were consistent then each shot should have blanketed one another, each shot patterning in the exact same spot. This may take a series of attempts, but with solid, correct gun mounts you'll develop a true pattern.

The math that Churchill followed is easy to understand. Every inch that the center of your pattern is off from the bull's-eye at 16 yards translates to a $\frac{1}{16}$-inch correction needed for your stock. This means that if the heart of your pattern was 4 inches left and 2 inches low, you need $\frac{1}{4}$-inch relief for cast, and the comb raised $\frac{1}{8}$ of an inch. This will create a centered pattern. Remember in this example you may want to raise the comb a full $\frac{1}{4}$ of an inch. This will create a 2-inch-high classic field pattern.

All of this might seem a bit more technical than you'd like to be about your shotgun, especially if it's a very lovely gun and you like it so much you think that it fits just fine. But throughout the process you learn the nuances of how a stock may or may not fit you. And learning these physical issues of the shotgun and your own shooting style will perfect your methods, and each measurement and improvement will bring you another step closer to matching the perfect gun to your style.

Think of gunfitting as similar to all the things you do to adjust the interior of your car to suit the way you drive and the way you sit in the driver's seat. All those adjustments are often a matter of inches, depending upon your physique. But getting a proper sight picture from your side-view and rearview mirrors makes a world of difference.

Side-by-Side versus Over-Under

The merits of a side-by-side versus an over-under have been debated in sporting magazines, books, and on bar stools for years. The purists prefer the side-by-side, and the modern shooter touts the over-under as the better gun. Whichever style you favor is more a question of personal preference rather than technical advantage.

However, when speaking of matters of gunfit there are some subtle differences between side-by-sides and over-unders. One widely held opinion is that over-under guns tend to shoot higher than side-by-sides. This is because of a phenomenon known as "muzzle flip." Side-by-sides and over-unders react differently to recoil. A side-by-side tends to have a more downward thrust, or muzzle flip, as a reaction to recoil. There is a certain amount of

The merits of a side-by-side versus an over-under have been debated in sporting magazines, books, and on bar stools for years.

flexure that occurs when firing a side-by-side that propels the shot string slightly lower. In response to this, many shooters are fit with a straighter comb when using a side-by-side.

This flexure that occurs in side-by-sides seems to be stabilized somewhat by the barrel configuration of an over-under. The thrust is more upward on an over-under, especially when the top barrel is fired. Because of the higher profile of an over-under, the muzzle flip is more prevalent on the top barrel compared to the bottom. This lesser barrel flexure combined with the higher profile of the top barrel contributes to an over-under shooting slightly higher.

Side-by-sides and over-unders can also react differently to cast. Over-under guns react negatively to extremes in cast. Excessive cast in an over-under pulls the heel of the stock out of alignment with the plane of the barrels. This can cause uncomfortable recoil and an inaccurate shot swarm. This is not so prevalent in a side-by-side because some cast off can actually line up the heel of the stock with the right barrel.

In my experience, some shooters need more cast when shooting a side-by-side compared to an over-under. Some shooters will line up the eye on the left barrel rather than the rib as the mount is complete. A little extra cast can provide more relief for the eye to center down the rib, rather than hanging up on the left barrel. Although this is less common, excess cast is not as problematic when handling a side-by-side.

The most obvious difference between an over-under and a side-by-side is the sighting plane. Looking down a side-by-side, there is a much wider sighting plane because the rib lies between the two barrels. This creates much more mass at the end of the gun. For some this can be distracting, particularly as the mount is completed and the barrels are lifted up into the line of sight. Others seem to be comforted by this mass at the end of the gun and can point and swing a side-by-side more accurately.

An over-under has a single sighting plane. The rib rests on top of the barrels rather than between them. This creates a slimmer profile at the end of the gun. A single sighting plane is less dis-

A side-by-side tends to have a more downward thrust, or "muzzle flip," as a reaction to recoil.

tracting for most shooters because there is less mass at the end of the gun. Today most competitive clay shooters favor over-under shotguns. Some clay-shooting games allow the gun to be pre-mounted. In this case a single sighting plane is much less distracting, making it easier to focus on the target. Also, the flight path of the clay is known in most clay shooting games. This creates a greater temptation to aim with the bead and barrel when lining up with the target. For some shooters, referencing the end of the gun without actually aiming is much easier with a single sighting plane.

There are obvious differences between hunting birds and competitive clay shooting. So why do some wingshooters prefer the side-by-side and most clay shooters use the over-under? In the field, game birds are unpredictable. They can appear in a flash and dart through the air with the acrobatics of a fighter jet. This forces you to swing your gun with your body spontaneously during the gun mount. The best wingshooters point at the bird as they smoothly swing the gun up to the shoulder and cheek. The mass at the end of a side-by-side helps them swing with the bird but is not distracting because of the reaction time of game shooting, and everything happens instinctively. In clay shooting, you can set up the body in advance to ensure the easiest angle needed to break the clay. There is more time in a clay shoot to develop a lead picture. Most clay shooters calculate lead more so than the wingshooter, but they still need to see the target clearly. Thus the single sighting plane of an over-under is less distracting and often preferred by most clay shooters.

In my experience a side-by-side needs a more precise fit than an over-under, although I don't have any statistics to back up this claim. But a side-by-side does seem a much less forgiving gun in terms of gunfit. An ill-fitting over-under is often much easier to handle than a poorly fitted side-by-side. I have conferred with other instructors and gunfitters on my hypothesis and they all tend to agree that a side-by-side does demand a more precise fit.

Whichever type of bird gun you choose to shoot it should be fitted to suit your build and shooting style. The fit of the gun is much more important to the wingshooter than the type of gun. Most shooters seem to worry about engraving and wood character more than fit. Just remember the prettiest shotgun in the world won't improve your shooting one bit if it does not fit you properly. In my time as an instructor, I've seen plenty of people miss again and again with the most gorgeous gun in their hands, and then see a shooter with a well-fitted, midlevel gun smack clays and knock down birds left and right.

Barrel Length

What about barrel length—how does that affect gunfit? Most barrel length is a personal preference, but the fit of your gun may influence how long your barrels should be. Many upland bird hunters prefer slightly shorter barrels that are easy to point and shoot. A short-barreled gun may feel lighter and quicker to mount in thick bird cover. However, many duck and dove shooters tend to favor longer-barreled guns. A longer-barreled gun will add more weight at the muzzle and will tend to swing easier. A 30-inch barrel will certainly feel more "muzzle heavy" than a 26-inch-barreled gun.

Length of pull should be a factor to consider when choosing barrel length. The general rule of thumb is to choose a barrel length that complements your length of pull. If someone has a 15¼ inch length of pull, then longer barrels may help to balance out the gun. If 13½ inches is your length of pull then you probably don't want 32-inch barrels on your upland bird gun. I have a 14¾ length of pull on my bird gun and tend to prefer 28-inch barrels. Anything less than that feels whippy to me. I find short-barreled guns difficult to point and swing. The gun comes up unevenly into the shoulder and cheek. I recently had 32-inch barrels fitted to my duck gun. This makes the gun a bit barrel heavy, which I like for pass shooting. So the type of shooting you'll be doing is also as much a factor as your length of pull when you choose your barrels. Your objective is to create a balanced bird gun that will swing and mount with ease.

Ribs

I have stated throughout this book that your focus should be squarely on the bird and not on the barrels. So why should anyone care about the rib on a gun? To be perfectly honest, the rib should have no real effect on your shooting. If the gun fits you, the eye and end of the barrel are in alignment. The rib simply runs on top of the barrels, or between the barrels on a side-by-side. That said, a less in-trusive rib will help a shooter maintain focus on the bird. Most field-grade guns have a thinner rib than a clay-shooting gun. This can help to reduce weight a little and be less distracting as the gun is mounted to the cheek and shoulder.

Note that many clay guns have a raised rib. This is especially true of trap guns. A raised rib is built up or slightly higher than the true sight line atop the receiver. If you raise the rib you effectively make the gun shoot lower. This would seem to be counterproductive when shooting trap because the birds are always rising. Most sporting clay shooters tend to prefer a flatter shooting gun. This means the pattern is dead centered, so a raised rib is often used to help lower the shot. The field shot tends to prefer a pattern that is slightly higher, and for this reason a raised rib is not favored on most bird guns.

My favorite rib on a bird gun is a Churchill rib. This type of rib is thicker near the receiver and tapers down and becomes thinner toward the bead. Churchill, as a gun maker, favored shorter barrels; however, his tapered rib design creates the illusion of longer barrels. I prefer this kind of rib because its tapered lines can make short-barreled bird gun seem longer.

That leads us to the bead on the end of the barrels. Your bird gun should have a small, low-profile bead. Using the bead to make sure of your alignment is totally useless when shooting game because in the heat of the moment there is no time to line up the eye with the bead. Some shotguns have a front and rear sight. A premounted clay shooter will use this to create the "figure-eight" sight picture. This allows the shooter to premount the gun the same way every time. The wingshooter does not have time nor is it an advantage to premount the gun. By fitting the stock properly you are assured that the eye and barrel relationship is perfect, so there is no need to aim.

I have seen too many shooters come to a shooting lesson with a Raybar sight attached to the end of their gun. A Raybar sight is ½ inch long and Day-Glo orange. Can you image anything more distracting? This type of sight actually makes seeing the bird all the more difficult. I recommend having one small pebble of a bead on the end of your bird gun. This is less distracting and makes it easier to focus on the bird.

Balance and Weight

Conventional wisdom says that a shotgun should balance out on the hinge pin. But that's not entirely true. A number of personal factors determine the balance point of a shotgun. The clay shooter might favor a balance point that is slightly forward of the hinge pin. This could help to create a more effortless follow-through, as the weight is slightly forward. The same could be said of a game gun for pass shooting waterfowl or for shooting high-flying pheasants. An upland gun for quail or grouse might have the balance point slightly behind the hinge pin. This can make the gun feel quick and easy on close-range birds. You can change the balance point by hollowing out some wood from the stock or by adding lead putty somewhere inside the stock. You could also add some lead tape to the inside of the forend. Depending on how you want to change the balance point there are a number of ways to do so, but you might want to seek the help of a professional gunsmith.

Conventional wisdom says that a shotgun should balance out on the hinge pin. The balance point of a shotgun is really a matter of personal preference.

The total weight of a bird gun can vary depending on the type of hunting you are going to do. This again is a question of personal preference. The upland shooter might want a lighter gun that is easy to carry in the field. The typical upland gun can range anywhere from 5½ to 6½ pounds. This can be more or less, depending on the gauge you choose. A .12-gauge shotgun for duck hunting can be around 7½ to 8½ pounds depending on the make and model. A lighter gun will be easier to carry and maybe quicker to shoot for upland game. A heavy gun swings smoothly and creates an effortless follow-through. You can't stop the momentum of a long-barreled, heavy gun as easily as with a lighter gun. A heavy gun also tends to absorb the effects of recoil.

I use a 12-gauge over-under for most of my clay shooting. I can't remember what it weighs, but I would say it's around 7¼ pounds, a pretty heavy gun. This is a great gun to putt a hundred rounds through in an afternoon on the clays course, but I wouldn't want to lug it around the woods all day. The extra heft makes the gun feel solid and target loads won't kick the gun into your shoulder. Because this gun is heavier than average, the lighter target loads are partially absorbed by the weight of the gun. This last season, however, I did most of my upland hunting with a nice little .28-gauge over-under. I got a good price on it from another instructor who didn't use it much any more. The stock naturally had a little cast on, which was good for me, being a lefty shooter. But the gun is also light enough to carry through the brush without it weighing me down. I had no trouble carrying it on long walks through some bigger coverts, which would have been a bit more arduous had I been carrying a heavy .12-guage. Overall, the weight of the gun should be suited to the job it is designed for. As

Post hunt tailgating with a bit of sloe gin.

a general rule, lighter guns are best for game shooting, especially when you're doing a lot of walking in thick cover, and heavier guns are best suited for clay shooting.

Stocks

There are many different types of stocks and grip styles to choose from. What type is best for the wingshooter can depend on a number of variables. Most upland guns are fitted with an English, or straight, grip. The English grip with its slim profile is lightweight and easy to point. The English stock is at its best on double-trigger side-by-sides. I prefer an English grip on a side-by-side because it puts both hands on the same plane when mounting the gun. Because the barrels are next to each other, a straight grip puts the grip hand up higher and in line with the lead hand on the forend. A full pistol grip on a side-by-side can hold the trigger hand lower than the plane of the barrels. This can create a seesaw gun mount, because the hands begin to work independently. Also, a straight grip allows you more freedom in where you wrap your hands around the grip. This can be useful on a double trigger when you need to reach each trigger precisely. A semi-pistol grip, however, can work on a side-by-side especially when it is matched with a single-trigger, box-lock-style gun.

A pistol grip is best on an over-under. I like the look and feel of a pistol grip on .12-gauge over-unders. This grip style can add control to the bulk of a .12-gauge gun. A semi-curved or even an English grip can be elegant on subgauge guns. This looks tasteful and a slimmer profile grip can really complement a .20- or .28-gauge gun.

Also there are comb and stock styles to consider. A classic field comb with a traditional stock really complements a fine bird gun. Other bulky stock configurations such as a Monte Carlo stock or parallel combs are truly for clay shooting. A parallel comb has a drop at comb and heel that are the same. Typically the dimensions on a parallel comb are $1\frac{5}{8} \times 1\frac{5}{8}$ inches. This creates a high drop at heel, but this can also reduce felt recoil a bit. This is because the heel is more in line with the barrels. Some traditional field stocks might have drops that are $1\frac{1}{2}$ inches at comb and $2\frac{1}{4}$ inches at the heel. Depending on length this often creates about $1\frac{5}{8}$ inches in drop at face, which is the same drop at face as the parallel comb described above. So avoid any gimmicky stock designs, especially one with an adjustable comb. The wingshooter needs a traditional

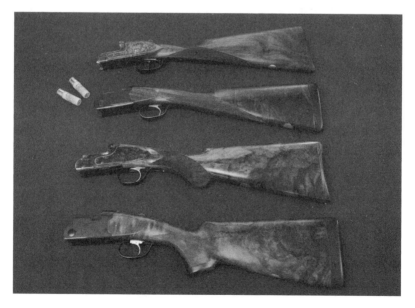

There are many different types of stocks and grip styles.

stock that fits. This will allow you to mount the gun with confidence and shoot more consistently.

Barrel Regulation

On higher-quality shotguns barrel regulation is not a concern. Most guns are regulated at 40 yards. This means that the pattern of each barrel should perfectly overlap each other at 40 yards. If this is not the case, this can lead to real problems for the shooter. It is best to test out a new gun to be sure that you are off to a clean start. You'll do best to have your barrels checked by an experienced gunsmith if you suspect any problems, rather than base any conclusions on your own visual inspection. If you suspect that you have a gun with barrels that are truly off, there is little that gunfitting can do to fix this problem because it is inherent to the gun. In such a case, you'll have to speak with the manufacturer or a very good gunsmith.

CHAPTER
FIVE

True Lessons from the Orvis Shooting School

What a job—teaching people how to break clay targets with a shotgun. I can't really call it a job, because a job is working for a paycheck. Coaching at the original wingshooting school in America and hunting for woodcock on your lunch break is more of a lifestyle than a job. Rather, it's a nice life. In my ten-plus years at the Orvis Fly Fishing and Shooting Schools I've made some great friends and met some wonderful people. The students do really make the schools interesting. My fellow instructors and I run basically the same program three times a week, and the students bring the variety and energize even the crusty veteran instructors. I've coached everyone from captains of industry to carpenters and everyone between, and every pupil presents particular challenges to my teaching ability. They keep me on my toes, and keep me honest.

I remember this one interesting student from California who was a piano tuner. His friend attending the school with him told me that he was world renowned for his precision and ability to create the perfectly harmonized piano. I wondered how I might somehow capitalize on his tuning abilities to create some kind of analogy to help him with his shooting.

"Think of how a properly tuned piano wire sounds—I mean, it almost *feels* natural," I said. "When your body is moving in harmony with the gun, you'll feel the same kind of 'being in tune.'"

The fellow looked at me and said, "I think that's a mixed metaphor, but I'll try to believe it."

He shot well, although we both concluded that I'd never learn to play the piano.

So many different kinds of people with such widely differing skill levels come to Orvis for shooting lessons, that over the years our coaches develop a keen eye. I've learned that a good coach is observant and listens well. In fact, the best coaches listen as much as they talk. Reading body language and listening are skills all great coaches have. This way they understand how the instruction should be given. Good coaches know what to say. Great coaches know how to say it.

Let me relate some true stories from my years as a wingshooting instructor and gunfitter. There are common pitfalls to avoid that happen in just about every school. These are typically not very serious problems and can be easily fixed. Also, I hope to give you some insight into what our very best students do well. Watching you shoot your best after diligent practice is a real treat. Often our returning students really get into the zone. You can learn from this and greatly improve your own skills if you study the habits of expert shooters. And if you're a new instructor, some of the anecdotes and stories here might help you develop your teaching abilities.

Let's first begin by avoiding some of the pitfalls that affect so many shooters in our schools. This is a short list of some of the more common problems that pop up all the time at the Orvis Wingshooting Schools.

A Deer Hunter's Old Habits

At the beginning of a teaching session at Orvis, we instructors always survey the crowd to get a sense of everyone's experience level. Then we try to group together the students according to skill level.

One year, I had an older couple named John and Sally in my class. John had just sold his business, and he and his wife were getting ready to retire early. Sally had an interest in shooting. She had never shot a shotgun before, but loved the idea of hunting on some of the land that her granddad had left her down South (her granddad had been an avid quail hunter). John was an avid deer hunter and had twenty-plus years of shooting experience, but sitting in a deer stand all day wasn't Sally's idea of fun. Bird hunting seemed like the perfect hobby for them to enjoy together.

We sometimes separate husbands and wives, as we jokingly say to the spouses, "One coach per group is enough." But John and Sally wanted to shoot together and they seemed like they could handle it, so I let them.

Guess who broke the most targets that first session? Sally. John struggled and hit only a few. Having rifle hunters struggle is common at the shooting school. Often the student with little or no shooting experience has more success than those with a lot of rifle shooting under their belt.

When John and Sally got to my station for their afternoon session you could clearly see something was brewing inside John. He was a self-made guy, a real doer, and, like most men, he believed he was born knowing how to shoot a gun. Hitting these little clay birds shouldn't be so hard. The more he missed, the harder he pressed, and Sally's great shooting wasn't helping his concentration.

With most type A males, the more they miss the harder they try. But breaking old muscle memory can be hard, particularly if you have years of experience shooting a certain way. Once John started to miss regularly he began to aim as if his life depended on it. Focusing too much on the end of the gun is disastrous when shooting a shotgun at fast-flying clay.

Once put under stress we revert to what is comfortable. The combination of John missing a few and Sally hitting everything caused him to fall back on old habits. The more he missed the harder he aimed. He was hunting for the clays—I could clearly see that he was aiming with his barrels as he pulled the trigger. When someone aims, the eye focuses on the barrels and bead, and the swing is stopped. The gun literally comes to a halt as the eye switches focus from the target to the barrel. As the gun stops, the target gets away and the miss is usually behind or low.

The target we started shooting at was a soft-paced, slightly right-to-left bird. I asked John where he thought he was missing. He said, "Behind, and I think a little low," and he was right. How could he know that? By the time his eyes went from the target to the barrels, the gun stopped and he could see the bead was behind the target. He didn't trust that the gun would shoot where his eyes were looking. He could either switch his focus back to the target or lead this very easy target by a mile. The latter of these two options is certainly not the way to go; pulling out ahead of the target and stopping the gun is a difficult way to consistently shoot.

On the next shot I told him to forget about the gun and focus hard on the clay. "Once you clearly have the clay in focus, just pull the trigger," I said.

On the next shot the barrels moved right with the target, but at the last second John aimed and missed again!

"You didn't trust it. At the last second you aimed again," I told him.

"Yes. How do you know that?"

I told him I could see the barrels stop when he aimed. He continued to miss so we tried something different.

"On this shot, John, when you see the target clearly, I'll say 'bang,'" I said. "You just focus on the bird and I'll tell you when to shoot. Your job is to look at the target. I'll know when your eyes are on the target by the movement of the gun, and that's when I'll say 'bang.' Trust it."

As the clay went out, his swing was perfectly in harmony with the flight of the bird. When his timing was right, I calmly said, "Bang," and he pulled the trigger. The clay burst into a cloud of orange smoke and little bits. John looked shocked and surprised. "Wow," he said. Right then the light went on for him. Calling the shot for him was a simple teaching trick, but it changed everything about his approach.

For the next hour he blasted the clays out of the sky. Over the course of the school he would miss a few and confess that he aimed and he would quickly remedy that.

I have seen this story play out hundreds of times. The rifle shooters have the hardest time letting go of that instinct to aim. Part of learning to wingshoot effectively is learning to trust your eye-hand coordination and the fit of your gun. The more you can focus on the clay the smoother your swing and mount become.

Granddad's Gun Isn't Always the Right Gun

One student of mine named Bill showed up for the start of school holding a few weathered leather gun cases. He looked like the typical New England bird hunter: he wore tattered hunting pants, a red hunting shirt, and a beat-up blaze-orange baseball cap. The season was set to begin in a few weeks, so I introduced myself and asked him if he thought it was going to be a good year. He was hopeful, but his workload didn't allow for too much scouting.

I began to inspect his guns. Orvis instructors always do a safety check and measure the guns that students bring to the school. This way we know if they're in good working condition, and we can get an idea of the stock dimensions.

Bill opened one of his cases and began putting together a nice older-model side-by-side. He spun around and handed me a sweet little Parker.

"This was my dad's grouse gun," he said proudly. Many of our students come to the school with an old gun that was passed on to them by their dad or granddad. It's usually an older side-by-side that they hope to use for bird hunting just as their forbears did. Bill also had a newer Beretta .20-gauge over-under that I took a look at.

Next we began to measure his guns to see how they fit.

"I assume that the Parker doesn't fit me very well, because I can't shoot worth a damn with that gun," Bill said.

I had a pretty good idea why the Parker was giving him fits and why he shot better with the Beretta. After we put the drop stick to the guns I gave him the stats.

"The Parker has a lot more drop than the Beretta. It can be tough to shoot a gun that has more drop than the shooter needs," I said, trying to be respectful of Bill's love for the gun. Early-model American-made side-by-sides often have excessive drop compared to today's average stock dimensions.

Next I had Bill mount each gun to get an idea of how he moved with them. He started with the Parker, taking the gun from the ready position and then smoothly mounting the gun to the shoulder and cheek. I could tell right away that he had good style. He held the gun alertly and mounted the gun perfectly. I asked him to hold the gun in the mounted position so I could check things out. Obviously, the gun indeed had too much drop for Bill because his right eye was looking into the back of the receiver.

Bill shot with both eyes open. He was right-eye dominant and right-handed, however, so keeping both eyes open was most likely not a problem.

I asked him to mount the gun again. Once he completed his mount I had him close his left eye.

"Can you see the rib or the bead?" I asked.

"No. My eye is looking into the back of the gun."

Hoping for something positive, I asked him to put down the Parker and pick up the Beretta, mount it, and close his left eye. He told me what I suspected: "I can see right down the rib on this gun," Bill muttered with a stock pressed into half his mouth.

"Can you see the bead as well?" I questioned.

"Sure can."

As I gave a quick glance you could see that his eye was sitting over the barrels much better on his over-under than with the side-by-side.

"Man, it has been driving my crazy why I couldn't shoot that Parker!"

I told him this was just a spot observation and that his gunfitting would tell us more. With the try gun we did a little more experimenting. We then patterned both his guns, and he could clearly see why he shot better with that one gun.

The Parker patterned very low and way left. His over-under patterned right on, but just a hair left. The numbers we came up with in his fitting with the try gun closely matched the dimensions of his Beretta. He just needed a little more cast in his over-under; otherwise it would have been perfect.

Bill's story is not uncommon. A gun that has too much drop can be very problematic. If a gun has excessive drop, particularly at the comb, the eye cannot peer correctly down the barrel. Some shooters learn to shoot a gun with too much drop by not fully mounting the gun to the cheek; they halfway mount the gun to the shoulder, but hold the head high. This way the eyes can sight down the rib. This is obviously bad form, but it can work. The real problem comes when such shooters pick up another gun. The half mount they have learned does not allow them to correctly handle a gun with less drop. This head-high mount can lead to other problems and must be avoided.

For Bill, his attachment to his dad's gun was sentimental. He wanted to bird hunt with the gun just like his dad had done before him, but he wanted the gun to fit him. He didn't care if alterations hurt the resale value of the gun, because he would never sell it. He was hoping someday to pass it on to his kids.

After school Bill left the Parker in the care of the Orvis gunsmiths. He invested in a nice piece of highly figured walnut and couldn't wait to see the finished product.

I didn't see Bill until the next year when he returned for another session of school. He took out his retooled Parker from the same old beat-up case. It really looked spectacular. Just few of us were standing in the gun room. For a few moments we all acted like little boys again who had just received a new baseball mitt for Christmas.

The new stock was built to Bill's measurements, so I had no surprise when he shot it superbly throughout the school. That year he sent me a Christmas card telling me how much he enjoyed hunting with his dad's old gun. The time and expense of rebuilding a stock is not something everyone wants to do, but for some it can help to pass on a family tradition and create years of hunting memories.

The lesson for the instructor here is to be respectful of your students' desire to use a family firearm, and to also be candid about the problems this particular kind of gun might pose. You might have to break the news that your student simply will not shoot very well with Dad's, Granddad's, or Great-Grandma's .20.

Fit Before You Buy

In anticipation of attending a shooting school, many people buy a new gun. This would seem to make perfect sense, but it can also be a pitfall.

Two former students of mine, Rod and Janet, were a young couple who had brought an English setter puppy to school with them. They hoped to hunt over their new dog and Janet was taking on the task of training her. The setter was such a nice-looking dog she made you consider getting another bird dog yourself.

Along with their dog, Rod and Janet brought a brand new set of guns: a nice pair of over-under shotguns. Rod bought a .20 for himself, and Janet opted for a .28 gauge. But right from the start I had my reservations about these shotguns.

Janet's gun at a glance seemed OK on her. However, I could tell right away that Rod's gun did not fit him.

I carefully questioned them about their new shotguns, a bit worried that their excitement to start shooting was about to become much reduced. Rod seemed to hint that he had taken the recommendation of a friend and picked out these guns at a local dealer. Rod thought that they had made the right choice by going with a .20 gauge for himself, and a .28 for Janet. I assured him that this was fine, but we wanted also to be sure that the guns fit reasonably well. He looked at me a little puzzled, as if this were something he had already considered. I explained the issues of fitting to him, and he grew concerned. I assured him that after the fitting we would have a better idea of how well their guns suited them.

During the first shooting session I had Janet in my group. Her gun fit her reasonably well. She had not shot much, but she was a natural. As she mounted her .28 gauge, it came up easily to the shoulder and cheek. She was busting clays left and right, and the gun was shooting right where her eyes were looking. After her fitting, the numbers indicated nearly a perfect match with her new gun. She was happy to hear this because she was shooting so well with her new gun that she would have been hard put to part with it after so much initial success.

Unfortunately, Rod had a little more trouble getting going with his gun. He was a big guy, and his gun simply did not have enough length or drop for him. As a result his eye was sitting too high in relation to the sight line of the barrels. This was causing him to shoot high. For the first few shots he missed very high over the clay. So I told him to try to miss a shot under.

"You mean you want me to shoot under the target?" Rod said.

"Miss *under* the target by a good bit."

"OK," he said in disbelief.

On the very next shot he shattered the clay. As soon as he broke the target he looked shocked.

"I was way under that one. I can't believe I hit it," he said.

I told him to shoot a few more, and we saw the same result. He hit every one, but his focus was clearly under the clay. His gun was not shooting where his eyes were looking. The bird we were shooting was not very hard, a soft 25- to 30-yard quartering shot. But I told Rod that hitting the clay with his poor gunfit would only get harder on faster and longer shots. By having to aim so low to break the clay, he began to realize that the farther away the target went the more off his pattern would be.

During his fitting we patterned his gun and he could clearly see that it was patterning very high and a little left. Rod was taller and bigger than most guys, while most guns stocks are made for an average man. He had bought his gun with the best of intentions, but he clearly saw that it was not right for him.

"What can I do to make this gun fit me?" he said.

"This is where it gets a little tricky," I explained. He could have some stock work done to his gun, but this was probably not a good idea. The stock work would probably cost as much as the gun was worth. This was not the best news, but Rod had no real attachment to the gun. He had no problem selling it and looking for something that was a better fit. "If I had known, I would have waited until after the fitting to buy a gun," he said.

The idea of putting $1,000 dollars in custom adjustments into a gun that costs $1,500 is not really practical. Yet so many people don't really consider the fit of a gun when they go to make a purchase. You wouldn't dream of buying a $1,000 suit without having it tailored. The same should hold true of a shotgun. I'm not saying that you must buy an expensive bespoke gun. However, you should have a session with a try gun before you buy a new or used gun.

CHAPTER

S I X

Traits of
Top Shooters

The Ready Position Has
Become a Natural Posture

I once shot with a friend (I'll call him Fred to spare him ridicule) who had a pretty good swing and mount but had a terrible ready position: his barrels often pointed skyward. He had good concentration and hand speed, and half of the time managed to race his shotgun to his shoulder and hang on long enough, and focus tightly enough, to knock down five or ten or twelve birds. Sure, he had some quail for the deep fryer, but his basic stance form was abysmal. I couldn't stop myself from coaching him.

You can often spot Orvis alumni very quickly by their setup and ready position. A signature of our teaching method is the stylish ready position, and our alumni routinely look the same: the gun is held alertly and the stance is balanced with the correct foot placement. They just look prepared to take the shot. You can almost tell that they are going to hit the target before the clay is launched.

I fixed Fred's terrible stance by working on his feet and his hands. I got his left hand properly placed on the forend; this hand grips the forend just about where it should when the trigger finger pulls, although it might slide ahead just a bit with some shooters. I also got him to stop all movement in his right hand, which he had taught to yank quickly on the stock to get mounted. This muted the seesaw action of his quick draw. Then I made sure he learned how to walk in a way that kept him aware of his foot placement: stride evenly, walking directly, not lazily or with any shuffle. If he was slightly out of stance when the dogs got birdy, he learned to take a step or two to put his feet in the right position, and at the same time to bring the shotgun up to the ready position rather than hold the gun in such a lax fashion that he used up too much time getting it to his shoulder.

Developing a Correct Lead Becomes Instinctive

Learning to shoot instinctively as the best wingshooters do is the key to success, but much of it can be misunderstood. The biggest misconception is that instinctive shooting has no built-in lead picture. This is really not true. Instinctive shooting does not require you to shoot right at the bird on every shot. The best wingshooters build the lead into their technique. The key fact to remember is that instinctive shooters *picture the lead without measuring it with the gun barrels*. I have hunted with many good shooters in some great destinations, and the one thing that I have noticed is that all expert shooters swing out ahead of the bird when needed.

However, if you ask them how much they lead the bird, the answer is almost always, "I don't know." They picture the lead without being hung up on how much of a lead it is. They use their swing and shot string to effectively take down the bird.

My favorite place to coach skilled shooters is at the high tower. There, on longer crossing shoots, you can truly see how good shooters swing ahead of the bird without deliberately aiming with the barrels. The clay shooter often gets the same shot ten times in a row, while the bird hunter rarely gets the same shot twice a season (unless maybe you're shooting dove in South America). So having a technique that allows you to instinctively develop the correct lead picture, time and time again in the field, is key because it enables you to deal with the unpredictability of wild birds. The hunter doesn't have the time to check his aim and shoot. You must focus exclusively on the bird and stay with the bird; your technique must be able to allow you this intense, exclusive focus on a grouse, pheasant, or quail.

Visual Concentration and Focus on the Target Are Unshakable

Without a doubt the best shooters all have a heightened sense of focus and visual concentration. This does not mean that they have the best vision. Rather, the peak performers all concentrate hard on the bird and block out the rest. One of my best students described it this way: "When I see the clay bird, I see very clearly a spinning orange disk against a curtain of brown and green. I don't see any trees." Some of the best shooters I have coached wore corrective lenses. I can remember one guy in particular from Texas who had very thick eyeglasses, but he could flat out shoot. When you shoot well, you don't even realize that your eyeglasses are on your face.

Knowing what to look at and how to heighten your focal concentration can be learned. Often the more experienced shooter can block out distractions and lock in on the target. I love to ask shooters who are on a run and blasting everything in sight what they are thinking about after they have just hit ten clays in a row. The answer is almost always, "I wasn't thinking about anything. All I remember is seeing and breaking the bird." This sounds easy enough, but how do you really do that?

First, you commit the fundamentals to muscle memory. Often when I'm coaching students I will tell them not to worry about the misses when we are working on something important. If their gun mount is off, then we will do some drills to perfect bringing the stock up to the shoulder and cheek. Once the mount is corrected we can redirect our focus on the target.

To heighten your visual concentration you must narrow your focus. On a miss we tend to see everything: the trees, clouds, and the gun barrel. On a hit the focus is narrow, and you can clearly see the bird fall from the sky or the clay exploding into a million pieces. When shooters are struggling, especially on an easy target, I have my students intensify their focal point on something very particular on the clay. Often I ask them to look at the rings on the clay or the leading edge and observe nothing else. The next shot is often a smashing success.

If you truly trust that your gun is shooting where your eyes are looking then focusing on the target becomes much easier. Once you begin to second-guess things, you begin to lose both your concentration and your focus on the bird. Thus, true concentration depends greatly on correct gunfit.

These three traits of the top shooters—the ready position, the correct lead, and focus and concentration—take a long time to develop into a wholly natural bodily movement that happens with absolutely no thought at all. These are your instincts, developed after proper gunfit. View them in the same way that a dog most likely *doesn't* think about getting birdy—they just happen naturally, instantaneously, and consistently.

Final Thoughts: Dogs & Gunfit

The romance of hunting birds is not just shooting your limit of wood ducks or grouse. The passionate bird hunter enjoys excellent company, a fine double gun, and a good dog. And I find that a proper gunfit has helped me live up to my end of the bargain when backing up another hunter, but especially when it comes to the dogs.

Like anyone else, I love my dogs. My dogs are smart enough to know when they make a mistake, or when I do. I can easily forgive a dog, but I don't like having my dogs have to forgive me. When a dog has done its job very well and gone on point perfectly to set you up for a good shot, you want to make it. Pulling off that shot fulfills a major part of your sporting relationship with your

A fresh snowfall on a Thanksgiving morning hunt in New England.

best friend, and your dog bringing a bird to hand is the conclusion of the act of hunter and dog.

Over time the dog and hunter learn how to work together. Before long they can read each other like a book, and their movements in the field become instinctively synchronized. So you certainly want to shoot your best when the dog does its part. Being at your best means that your gun is right—that it is tailored to your unique build and shooting style. This doesn't mean you have to spend a fortune on a Purdy. Having a gun fitted to you can sometimes be done rather easily and not at great expense. There are many more good shotguns out there than you can ever own, and many reasonable gun makers offer custom stock work for their customers. Finding the right bird gun happens when you get the gun to fit you, not the other way around.

Best of luck, and cheers to the sporting life.

Notes

1. Macdonald Hastings, ed., *Robert Churchill's Game Shooting: A Textbook on the Successful Use of the Modern Shotgun*, rev. ed. (London: Michael Joseph, 1970) Preface p. xix, xx.
2. Paul Fersen, The Orvis Catalog.
3. Churchill, *Game Shooting*, p. 35.
4. Churchill, *Game Shooting*, p. 44.
5. Churchill, *Game Shooting*, p. 45.
6. Churchill, *Game Shooting*, p. 208, 209.

Glossary

Butt or Butt Stock: The end part of the stock that meets the shoulder when the gun is mounted.

Cast: The degree to which the stock is bent right or left of the rib or barrels. "Cast off" is used to describe the stock being angled slightly to the right. "Cast on" is the term used when the stock is angled slightly to the left. Obviously, a right-handed shooter prefers cast off, and a left-handed shooter favors cast on.

Comb: The top line of the stock where the shooter places the cheek on the stock.

Drop at Comb (D@C): The distance from the comb on the top of the stock to the rib on the barrel.

Drop at Heel (D@H): The distance measured from the plane of the rib to the heel on the stock.

Drop, or Bend: The distance from the rib to the top line of the stock. Drop is composed of two measurements: drop at comb and drop at heel.

Drop Stick: A tool used to measure the drop at comb and drop at heel on a gun.

Heel: The part of the stock where the comb runs down and meets the butt of the stock.

Length of Pull (LOP): The distance from the middle of the trigger to the middle of the butt stock.

Pitch: The degree or angle at which the butt stock is cut in relation to the gun barrel.

Rib: The top line of metal on the top of the barrels.

Toe: The part of the stock at the bottom curve of the butt.

Try Gun: A shotgun action outfitted with a special stock that is fully adjustable; used by a gunfitter to find the ideal stock dimensions for an individual shooter.

Index